LIM
LEMON &
SARSAPARILLA

For Gillian

LIME, LEMON & SARSAPARILLA

THE ITALIAN COMMUNITY IN SOUTH WALES 1881-1945

COLIN HUGHES

seren

Seren is the book imprint of
Poetry Wales Press Ltd
Nolton Street, Bridgend, Wales
www.seren-books.com

First published 1991. Reprinted 2003
© Colin Hughes
Foreword © Victor Spinetti

ISBN 1-85411-083-7
A CIP record for this title is available
from the British Library

The publisher works with the financial assistance
of the Welsh Books Council

Printed in Plantin by Cromwell Press, Wiltshire

Contents

Illustrations

Maps

Foreword

One afternoon, in my father's chip shop at 47 Marine Street, Cwm at around 3 p.m., a charming young couple chatted amiably in Italian to my father.

I was nine years old at the time, for this was just before the outbreak of the Second World War. The young couple had come up from the Italian Consulate in Cardiff. They were proposing to give lessons to the children of Italian immigrants in the area on future Saturday mornings. What a pity, they said, that those children were not brought up to speak the language of their Italian fathers.

I would not have minded learning Italian, but I could only think of the horror of the extra school, and on a Saturday morning! The one morning of the week when all of us Valley kids flocked to the pictures to laugh with Laurel and Hardy, laugh at the Three Stooges and wonder at the adventures of Flash Gordon's trip to Mars.

My sulking and "pulling a face" the following Saturday morning earned me a clip on the ear as I was put on the bus to Ebbw Vale, where the Italian lessons were to be held. Dad had bought me a leather satchel, a pen, an exercise book and a bottle of ink, the cost of which could have kept me in Saturday morning pictures for the rest of my young life. I can still smell the mixture of ink and leather inside that satchel even today.

Our young lady teacher was very charming, telling us that as this was our first meeting, we would just get to know each other and that she would take the register, that is our names, at the next Saturday lesson. She chirruped on in the bright sunny room above Carini's chip shop in Ebbw Vale but my mind was elsewhere in the picture house, imagining what Flash Gordon was up to on his trip to Mars.

Suddenly I heard our teacher say that the best at their lessons would be taken to Italy to meet Mussolini, or in her glowing phrase "our beloved *Duce*". Her attempts at fascist propaganda went way above our heads. Now I knew that our dad was not allowed to go to Italy under the Mussolini regime even for his own father's funeral. Dad had no love for "*Il Duce*".

On my return home, when I was asked what we had done that morning, I said nothing much, except that the best at lessons would be taken to Italy to meet Mussolini, our beloved *Duce*. "You are never going there again" said dad, quietly and grimly, and I never did. So I was able to be taken prisoner once more by Hollywood for endless Saturday mornings to come.

This was one of the memories realised for me when I read this marvellously documented book, memories of those quiet, gentle people, the Italians who supplied warmth, somewhere to go, and comfort amidst the smell of freshly ground coffee and the taste of the sharp tang of Raspberry and Ice; cheerful, cosy havens for the folk of the sometimes windswept and rainwashed valleys of South Wales.

Victor Spinetti
Manchester, 1991

Preface

Conti's shop in Cefn Fforest stands, well placed for business, where two bus routes meet. Nearby, from the gable end of a terraced house, Stanley Baldwin, pipe in hand, gazes down: 'Vote for the National Government'. He'll be lucky. In the window of Conti's shop, Fry's Cream Bars, Five Boys chocolate, and 'Everlasting' strips of toffee stretch along the front from end to end. Behind rises a colourful display, a pyramid of boxes: Capstan, Star, and Woodbine cigarettes. In red and gold, beside the door, a mirror bears the legend: 'Temperance Bar'.

Inside, coal miners, newly scrubbed, stand idly in the outer room, talking and smoking. Two bend over a pinball machine; the nudge is gentle, but the 'Tilt' light ends their play. They curse. Young boys move among the taller figures hoping for the latest cigarette cards: a 'Champion of Sport' from the Park Drive smokers perhaps — Don Bradman for preference — or a 'Radio Celebrity' from Wills.

Along the counter, a glass cabinet displays a line of stemmed ice-cream dishes. On the shelves behind, centrally placed, stand three white, gold-banded, porcelain barrels gaily painted with pictures of peaches and grapes. Each bears the name of the liquid inside: lime, lemon and sarsaparilla. On either side, in serried ranks, are jars of quality wrapped sweets — Barker and Dobson fruit drops, Lovell's Toffee Rex ('The King of Toffees'), Pascall's Butter Whole Brazils, Nuttall's Mintoes — expensive delights for special days. The cigarettes are to the left, in a lockable cabinet with a pull down front to comply with Sunday trading laws.

A door leading from the outer room reveals a tiny room beyond with two small tables, where commercial travellers occasionally display their wares to Mr Conti or eat their eggs and bacon. Mrs Conti hovers at the entrance to the living quarters, behind the counter. After school, her boys will serve there and if you know them well as playground pals, you'll get an extra dab of ice-cream on your ha'penny cornet. The coffee machine hisses from time to time but not many can afford such luxury.

* * * * *

Those are my childhood memories. The Contis have long gone from Cefn Fforest to better things at Newport. The Basinis who followed them have also left. The Temperance Bar is a hair-dressing salon now. All down the valleys of South Wales the Italian cafés, once such a feature of the social life, are closing their doors. Not all have gone, and some will survive long into the future. But, for the most part, the third and fourth generations of Welsh Italians have turned their backs on catering and have entered the professions. Television has robbed the cafés of their evening customers and the Chinese takeaways are moving in. However, the Italian community in Wales still thrives and the links with Italy are strong.

This is the story of those who migrated from northern Italy to South Wales at the turn of the nineteenth century, leaving behind them poverty and deprivation in the mountains of Emilia Romagna to seek prosperity in the booming industrial valleys in South Wales. Most came from a relatively small area, the valley of the Ceno, of which the small and ancient town of Bardi is the commercial centre. With great tenacity, these migrants from a peasant background captured much of the catering trade in South Wales. Many prospered, notably the members of the Berni family, of present day 'Steak House' fame. Others got by with no great claim to fortune.

First came the pioneers in the café trade: the Bernis, Bracchis, Rabaiottis and others who established their own businesses in the last decade or so of the nineteenth century. They were not the first Italians in Wales — musicians, statue makers, and sailors preceded them — but they made the greatest impact on the social life of the native population and laid the foundation for the Italian community as it is today. Young boys — some no more than twelve years old — were then brought over in large numbers in the early nineteen hundreds to help in the café trades. They pushed hand carts around the streets to sell ice-cream, graduated to horse and cart, and then managed new establishments, on a profit-sharing basis, for their masters. As the boys grew older they set up places of their own and generally looked to Bardi for their wives. By the mid-193)s, there were more than three hundred Italian cafés in Wales.

In writing this history, I have tried to portray the Italian community against a background of developments and events in South Wales may have helped to shape it. In order to illuminate the social and economic life of the community, and its interaction with the native population, a close look is taken at a number of families in the Rhondda valleys, a part of Wales that was at the height of its industrial development when the first wave of immigrants arrived. This is a small sample, but parallels drawn with Italian families in other parts of South Wales, show that life in these Rhondda cafés was typical of that elsewhere.

I found very little written contemporary material relating to the early Italian arrivals in Wales — an account book here, and a school certificate or naturalisation certificate there. This may be due in part to the high level of illiteracy in Italy at the time, for even if the immigrants could write the chances were that people back at home could not read. I have, perforce, relied to a great extent on oral interviews with present members of the community. For the early years, much of the material collected in this way is second hand — recollections of tales that parents told — but I was fortunate in being able to interview some first generation immigrants who came to this country some seventy years ago.

For later periods, and for the second and third generations, first hand accounts were easier to find. A full list of interviewees and other contributors is given in the bibliography, but these entries cannot convey the warmth of the reception, and the generous hospitality, given to me by many people. In this respect, and at the risk of giving some offence through oversight, the following deserve special mention: Aldo and Ron Bacchetta of Porth; Ino and Edda Conti of Treharris; John and Lilliana Conti of Bassaleg; Pierino and Tina Cordani (née Melardi) of Aberaman; Alma Cushion (née Cordani) of Hengoed; Marco Fulgoni and Ida Pini of Pontypridd; Aldo and Mario Rabaiotti of Swansea; Vic and Nina Resteghini of Blackwood.

I am greatly indebted to Professor David Smith of the University of Wales College of Cardiff who supervised, and did much to shape, the studies on which this book is based. From the many Italians in Wales who gave so freely of their help, I must single out Ino Conti of Treharris, who spared no effort, in Wales and in Bardi to meet my many demands. Thanks are also due to Gino Rabaiotti and Millo Caffagnini for help from Bardi, to Professor Mario Damonte of the University of Genoa, to Patrick Hannan and Herbert Williams of the BBC, to Bernard Baldwin in Mountain Ash, to Lucio Sponza and Carole Adams in London, and to Professor Ieuan Gwynedd Jones in Aberystwyth.

I :
The Exodus

La su per le montagne,
Tra boschi e valli d'or.

(Up amongst the mountains,
In the woods and golden valleys.)
Song, 'La Montanara'

In winter, the people of the town number little more than four thousand, but in summer the figure rises sharply and spoken English, heavily accented, mingles with dialect Italian in the square. Cars with GB plates are everywhere, among them an occasional Rolls Royce. Their owners are not ordinary tourists, but *oriundi Bardigiani* — people of Bardi extraction — returning to the land their forebears left, two, three, or four generations ago. They greet alike old friends and relatives from Bardi and from Wales: Contis from Treharris and Newport; Rossis and Sidolis from Ebbw Vale; Basinis and Gazzis from the Rhondda Valley; Tambinis from Tonyrefail. Some have summer residences in Bardi, or in the area around, which gives the town prosperity; some stay with relatives. A few, among the older ones, will never leave again, choosing to enjoy remaining years in the Italian sun.

The small hill town of Bardi lies in the north west Apennines of Italy, where the mountains rise from the northern plain near the city of Parma in Emilia Romagna. The old houses of this once-fortified town cluster around an imposing nineth century castle, recently restored, poised on an outcrop of rock which dominates the broad, tree-clad, valley of the River Ceno below. The newer part of the

13

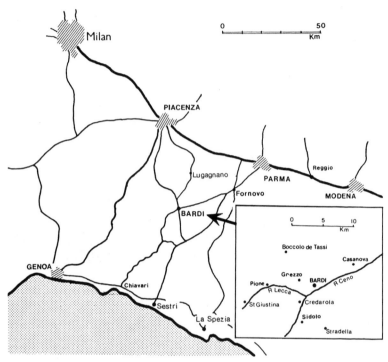

Map. 1 The Ceno Valley and northern Italy

town is little more than one long street, rising from the castle to a pretty square above. This is the market place; a focus for pavement café life. Here, in summer, men play at being the Government.

Bardi is the administrative centre of, and gives its name to, the surrounding *comune:* twelve *frazione*, or parishes, spread over an area of fifty-six square miles, from Santa Giustina in the west to Casanova in the east; from Boccolo de Tassi in the north to Stradella in the south. The view of the *comune* from the castle is breathtaking: the River Ceno sparkles in the sunlight; the road to Fornovo, and Parma beyond, winds far below; and tiny white villages dot the green hills. The tranquil valley has a prosperous look.

A hundred years ago it was very different. The castle then was crumbling; the little town was drab. In the communities around, peasants toiled on unproductive land. Oxen pulled the plough

1. Bardi in 1986, the town from the castle

2. The castle at Bardi

laboriously down the hill, but lacked the strength to cut an upward furrow. An ox was also used to pull around a sledge, carrying crops and other loads at less than human walking pace. Those who could not afford to keep an ox, used a cow — perhaps their only cow — to pull the sledge, and this was slower still.

Each village struggled to maintain its independence. The carpenter, the cobbler, and the stonemason in the village itself, and the blacksmith and the midwife close at hand, were no more prosperous than the peasants for whom they mostly did their work. Landless charcoal burners in the woods, from other parts of Italy, were poorer still. They built themselves small huts and lived there in the wood, near to their charcoal furnaces.

Everywhere, the pace was slow, the implements crude, the plots small; and the families were large. It could not last. Today, among the trees in remote parts of the *comune*, small, derelect hamlets can be seen. Stones still mark the boundaries of the tiny strips of land on which the peasants once struggled to make a living. Their primitive tools and sledges can still be found. Overgrown orchards and small patches of vine still produce their fruit, but the men who tended them left long ago.[1]

* * * * *

In the 1870s, nearly 60 per cent of the active population of Italy worked on the land.[2] The fertile northern plains, and a few productive coastal strips further south, were farmed intensively and gave a worthwhile yield; but increasing competition from abroad threatened their viability. Improved transport in the New World, and faster ships, brought imports pouring in: grain from across the Atlantic and rice and silk from the Orient. Imports of wheat more than trebled in the three years from 1884 to 1887.[3]

In southern Italy, malaria ruled the lowlands and the summer heat scorched the more tender crops. The peasants, mostly labourers, lived in the hills and tried to scratch a living from the arid land. Uncaring, absent landlords neglected to make investment in the land, or would not take the risk. The peasants starved.

In the Alpine and hill areas of the north, peasant land-owners, or their tenants, worked the fields and forests in small plots, as they did at Bardi. The land was poor, through lack of beasts or chemicals.

16

3. The derelict hamlet of Ronchi

They lived from hand to mouth. Some small land owners, unable to subsist on the products of their land, would also work as labourers in the more prosperous areas in the foot hills and the plains. The *mezzadria* system was also widely practised, by which a tenant provided tools and labour while the owner of the land paid rates and taxes, and gave seeds and plant and stock. No money rent was paid but the profits were divided half and half — as the word *mezzadria* implies — or often more in favour of the landlord. The *mezzadria* system had one great drawback: gains from an investment by one party had to be shared equally with the other. Tenants were reluctant to buy new tools or to invest in machinery; landlords drew back from supplying more vines, or trees, or animals. The stagnation which inevitably followed was compounded by the tendency for each peasant, whether owner or tenant, to cultivate a variety of products to meet his family's daily needs. Such a backward form of agriculture, with no specialisation in animals or crops, made for an independent and self-contained community, but one that was doomed to lasting poverty.[4]

To these long standing problems, the Government added more. To finance public works and industrial expansion, it levied higher

4. The Contis of Porelli in the parish of Crederola, near Bardi, 1897. The baby in white is Giuseppe Conti, later of Treharris.

taxes. These bore heavily on those with lower incomes and put a squeeze on agriculture. The industrial growth which followed was short-lived; it petered out in 1887 and ended with depression. It did nothing for the countryside. Although land and agriculture provided much of the revenue, it went mostly on investment on the railway and other public works, and on building up the armed forces and the government machine.[5] Little public expenditure took place in rural Italy, and the suffering was intense.

The government also introduced new laws of inheritance under which, on death, at least half of the estate had to be distributed equally among the children. Small farm holdings became even more fragmented and impossible to work. Strips of land owned by one individual were often widely separated, and access could be difficult, or even impossible, if families fell out. The impact of these laws was particularly marked in the northern hills, where holdings were already far too small. In the outer regions of the Ceno valley there are, today, run-down houses which continue slowly to decay because their many owners — all related — cannot agree on a scheme of renovation. [6]

Apart from a few large businesses in the northern regions, Italy in the 1880s was an industrially backward country. Enterprise was rare. Factories were few and the workforce mainly female. In the south, particularly, most workers were unskilled and worked in 'cottage' industries. Illiteracy was high: most people spoke the local dialect and nothing else. As little was written in dialect, the incentive to learn to read was slight. In 1881, in Italy as a whole, 62 per cent of those aged six and over were illiterate. There were large regional variations: in Calabria, in the south, the proportion of illiterates was as high as 85 per cent; it was lowest in Piedmont, the most industrialised region of the north, at 32 per cent. In Emilia Romagna, where Bardi lies, illiteracy was close to the national average, at 64 per cent.[7] In the hill schools, one teacher, one classroom for all age groups was the rule and children were given long holidays in summer to help around the farm. They left school when they were between ten and twelve years of age.

The picture of Italy in the latter part of the last century is therefore one of a poor and illiterate country, short of skills and capital. There seemed, at the time, little hope for improvement. For many, the only escape from this situation was emigration.

Emigration from Italy

Emigration from Italy was not new. It was common practice for peasants in the northern regions to take seasonal employment, mainly in the building trades, in France, Switzerland, and Austria-Hungary; and even before 1871 there was permanent emigration to countries as far away as South America, again mainly from the north.[8] There are also much earlier examples of residence abroad. There were Italian cafés in Paris as far back as 1670, and the owner of one of these, Tortini, is credited with the invention of ice-cream in the late eighteenth century.[9] A long history of Italian involvement in the café and ice-cream business was thus begun.

The Italian census for 1871 gave the number of Italians living abroad as four hundred thousand. This was almost certainly an underestimate as some countries refused to supply the relevent data on Italian immigrants. By 1891, the figure had risen to more than 1.4 million in the Americas alone. A flood had started: one hundred thousand a year were leaving for other European countries, and more than double that number for the Americas; and many of these were now coming from the south.[10] In 1901, it was estimated that three and a half million Italians out of a total population of thirty-three million were living abroad: three-quarters of a million in the United States; nearly two million in South America; and about six hundred and fifty thousand scattered throughout the European countries. In the following few years, emigration reached an annual total of half a million of whom, however, a large percentage returned: 37 per cent from the United States and 70 per cent from Argentina.[11] Those from Latin America were disenchanted. The attitude of the big landowners there — many of them Italian in origin — to their labourers was much the same as that of the big landowners in Sicily; many emigrants found they had leapt from the frying-pan to the fire.[12] At one point, the number of Italians leaving Latin America exceeded the number arriving. Many of those returning from the United States, however, were much more prosperous than when they left. Their poise and new-found independence were clear signs to those who had stayed in Italy that literacy paid. This was a greater spur to learning than any exhortation from Rome´and the general level of literacy steadily improved.[13]

The Italian government took no steps to discourage emigration: the remittances from those who found work abroad greatly eased the poverty of those they left behind, besides contributing to Italy's trade balance.[14] However, the Prime Minister, on a tour of the south, was shocked to be greeted by one town mayor "on behalf of the eight thousand people in the *comune*, three thousand of whom are in America and the other five thousand preparing to follow them."[15] Laws were passed in January 1901 to control the movement of emigrants, who were being exploited by unscrupulous ticket sellers, but no restrictions were placed on the numbers leaving. The protection of the government was also extended to Italian citizens abroad and the destitute were given a passage home. These provisions were, however, restricted to those travelling to countries beyond the Suez Canal or beyond the Straits of Gibraltar, excluding the coast of Europe. Many of the advantages were therefore denied to those going to Britain.[16]

Of course, the pattern of outflow was not determined solely by conditions on the land, nor by the attitude of the government. There was always the pull of a 'crock of gold' in another country and a desire to follow the example of those who had prospered. The emigrants went where prospects seemed best. Those from Bardi went to London and to Wales.

Emigration to England and Wales

In the period between 1871 and 1901, at least 80 per cent of the Italian migrants to England and Wales came from northern Italy. The northerners, of course, had less far to come than those from the south and could more easily afford the fare. They also had more abundant sources of information about conditions in Britain. Among those who came were organ-grinders from Emilia-Romagna and bar and restaurant owners from Piedmont and Tuscany. At first, London was the greatest magnet. Before the end of the nineteenth century, the Italian community in London had its own church, hospital and schools, and there were more than nine hundred ice-cream carts in this 'Little Italy' in Clerkenwell and Holborn.[17] This was a poor part of London with a high density of population. For those prepared to live in crowded buildings, accommodation was cheap, notwithstanding the area's proximity to the West End and the City. Manchester also exercised a pull and had its own 'Little Italy' in Ancoats.

The census returns give the following figures for the number of people of Italian birth in England and Wales[18]

1871	1881	1891	1901	1911	1921	1931
5063	6504	9909	20332	20771	20401	18792

The James Commission, which investigated 'the evils' attributed to alien immigration in 1903, had some doubts about the accuracy of census figures in respect of immigrants: "Positive accuracy is not to be found in census reports — an uncertain quantity should be added," they said in their report. However, they soon concluded that the census returns gave the "nearest approach" to the true figure and that other sources — for example Board of Trade shipping returns which showed that the numbers arriving annually at the ports had trebled in the previous decade — were less reliable.[19]

Whatever the imperfections in the census figures, the trend is clear. The number of Italian-born in England and Wales rose sharply between 1881 and 1901 and then levelled off, before declining slightly after 1921. This stabilisation was to some extent the result of the Aliens Act of 1905 which put restrictions on the entry of foreign workers into Britain. An increase in immigration in the years before the First World War was offset by the number of Italians returning to do military duty in the period 1915 to 1918.[20]

The 1881 census gives a detailed breakdown of the occupations of the Italians in England and Wales. Out of a total population of six thousand five hundred and four including women and those too young to work, a staggering twelve hundred and forty were musicians. These were mainly itinerant organ-grinders, this being a traditional occupation of Italian migrants. The more highly-regarded, but less numerous, Italian teachers of music would also have been included in this figure. Sailors were in the next highest category, although many, no doubt, were temporary visitors. There were five hundred and ten servants, three hundred and fifty-six street sellers and four hundred and sixty in the hotel, catering and confectionary trades (including one hundred and thirty non-domestic cooks). There were one hundred and thirty-four carvers or gilders, two hundred and forty-five 'image' makers, one hundred and seven paviours and twenty-four general labourers. In spite of the background of many, none seems to have gone into agriculture.

Migration to Wales

There were two hundred and forty-three people of Italian birth in Wales and Monmouthshire in 1871. This figure more than doubled in the next ten years, and by 1901 there were almost one thousand. There was then a steady increase to one and a half thousand in 1921; thereafter, the numbers declined, as they did for England and Wales as a whole.

The bulk of the Italians in Wales were concentrated in Glamorgan, with a high proportion of the rest in Monmouthshire, as the following table shows. Apart from a temporary influx into rural Cardiganshire in the early 1900s, which we discuss elsewhere, other Welsh counties had no more than a handful or two each. Some had none at all.

	1871	1881	1891	1901	1911	1921	1931
Glamorgan	*	455	511	684	833	997	*
Monmouthshire	111	89	31	89	303	335	*
Other W. counties	*	36	25	153	159	201	*
Total	243	580	567	926	1295	1533	1394

*County figures not given.

In Glamorgan, the number of Italians rose steadily from four hundred and fifty-five in 1881 to more than double that figure in 1921. The figures for Monmouthshire are erratic in the early years for reasons which are not explained in the census report; it may be that there was an unusually large number of sailors, or other visitors, in the county in 1871, or internal movement between Monmouthshire and Glamorgan. The figures do show, however, that the main influx into Monmouthshire took place between 1901 and 1911, despite the restrictions on entry introduced by the Aliens Act 1905.

One feature of the Italian population in Wales was the very high ratio of males to females: about ten to one in the period up to 1901 (see Appendix 1 for detailed figures). It is, of course, natural for immigrants to be unaccompanied in the early years of residence, but the ratio of men to women for England and Wales as a whole was only about three to one in the same period. This suggests that the Italian immigrants in Wales were generally much younger than those in England, and well below marriageable age.

The 1921 census report divides the number of Italians in Glamorgan into various occupational categories. Unfortunately the categories are too broad to be very revealing of small populations such as that of the Italians. For example, out of a total number of six hundred and fourteen occupied people, two hundred and twenty-one are recorded as being in commerce or finance; one hundred and eighty-four in undefined 'personal services'; and forty-two as makers of food, drinks or tobacco. All three categories could embrace the café and confectionary trades which are not separately identified. In addition, ten are shown in metal working, forty-eight in mining or quarrying, fifty-three in transport, and ten in building. Not one was employed on the land. The occupations of Italians in other Welsh counties are not recorded.

At first sight there is a surprising absence of ice-cream manufacturers and sellers in the Glamorgan figures for 1921 for we know from other sources that this was a major occupation of the Italians in South Wales at that time. Writing in 1926, J. Ronald Williams said, of Merthyr Tydfil: "There are fifty-two Italians here...They provide an interesting example of a body of people who come not to participate in industry, but to cater in the comestible luxuries of the working people. They almost monopolise the fish and chip and ice-cream business."[21] They continued to do so: by 1938 there were well over three hundred cafés in Wales and Monmouthshire, mostly in the mining valleys of the south, owned or run by Italian immigrants or their descendants.[22]

This illustrates another basic weakness in the census process. The data are collected at the end of March, or in early April, and even if an appropriate category existed for, say, ice-cream sellers, such summer seasonal work would not be recorded.[23]

Industrial Growth in South Wales

In sharp contrast to Italy, South Wales experienced rapid and prolonged industrial growth throughout the nineteenth century to become, at the end, one of the largest centres of heavy industry in the world.[24] The production of iron led the way, with major iron-works along the northern edge of the coalfield — Dowlais, Cyfarthfa, Penydarren and the 'Plymouth' works in Glamorgan; Blaenavon, Ebbw Vale and Rhymney in Monmouthshire — and smaller works, linked to tinplate manufacture, in the southwest.

For the first half of the nineteenth century, South Wales dominated the British iron industry, but increasing difficulties with the supply of local ore, and a switch in demand from iron to steel, the meeting of which required enormous investment, led to the closure of a number of the northern ironworks in the late 1870s. Nevertheless, many of the larger works successfully made the transition to steel. Dowlais was still a huge complex in the mid-1880s and was holding its own at the beginning of the First World War. It survived into the inter-war years, as did the works at Ebbw Vale.[25] It was to Merthyr and Ebbw Vale, the neighbouring towns of these large plants, that some of the early prospective café owners from Bardi found their way.

As the northern works declined, new steel enterprises sprang up along the coast, from Newport in the east to Port Talbot in the west, to take advantage of cheaper imported ores: a "Dowlais by the sea" at Cardiff in 1888; Nettlefold at Rogerstone and Newport in 1886; and Lysaght at Newport in 1896.[26] Further west, around Swansea and Llanelli, the tin-plate manufacturers also prospered as the consumption of canned food rose, and demand for their products increased. By then, however, coal had taken over as the dominant industry in Wales. The bituminous seams of Monmouthshire and east Glamorgan, the steam-coals between the rivers Taff and Neath, and the anthracite coals of Carmarthenshire and west Glamorgan were exploited, in turn, to meet demand from a variety of users. As the requirement for coal for smelting slackened, an explosion in demand for good steam-coal took place. In the 1880s, the conversion of the world's shipping from sail to steam gathered pace. The best steam-coal, the Admiralty decided, came from Wales, and others followed this advice. Between 1890 and 1910, the South Wales coalfield provided nearly one-third of all world exports of coal. At first the demand was met from the accessible seams around Aberdare but in the 1870s, when techniques had been developed to reach deep seams, the twin valleys of the Rhondda began to be aggressively exploited. Twenty three new collieries were opened in the Rhondda in a decade, and production continued to rise rapidly thereafter as even deeper seams were mined. While the Rhondda took over Merthyr's mantle as the leader of industrial growth, significant developments took place elsewhere across the coalfield: in the Ogmore and the Garw valleys; at Senghennydd and Aber-tridwr. There was even a resurgence in areas of previous decline. Hard on the heels of this race for steam-coal, came an unexpected upsurge in demand for anthracite, as new ways were found to burn it. Output from the anthracite mines of Carmarthenshire, Brecon-shire and west Glamorgan — long the Cinderella areas of the coal-field — trebled between 1894 and 1913.[27]

Arm-in-arm with these developments went a rapid growth in the railway network and a massive build-up in the ports. New docks were built at Cardiff — already the greatest coal port in the world — and the facilities at Newport, Swansea, Port Talbot and Llanelli were extended. The most enterprising development of all came in 1889, when the Rhondda coal-owners, frustrated by congestion and high tariffs at Cardiff, built new docks at Barry on a scale sufficient to challenge the supremacy of Cardiff. These were so successful that, in 1913, Barry superseded Cardiff as the largest coal-exporting port in the world.[28]

To fuel this extraordinary growth, people and capital poured into the industrial and commercial areas of South Wales. The popula-tion of Glamorgan doubled in the last thirty years of the nineteenth century and topped a million and a quarter in 1921. In 1800, it had been less than one hundred thousand. Monmouthshire, despite remaining rural in the east, also doubled its population over a relatively short period. It rose from less than two hundred thousand in 1871 to just under four hundred thousand in 1911.

Within these county trends there were some remarkable examples of high local growth: the population of the urban district of Barry doubled in just ten years following the building of the docks, and Mountain Ash was not far behind with an increase of more than 74

per cent in the same short period.[29] Labour was being drawn in
mainly from adjacent counties, and from other rural parts of Wales,
but also from England and Ireland, and from countries abroad,
attracted by high wages and the general excitement.[30] In 1911,
Cardiff was second only to London in the proportion of foreign-
born in the population, and of all the counties in England and
Wales, including the administratve county of London, Glamorgan
had the third highest number of Italians.[31]

In *Rhymney Memories*, Thomas Jones described the changes that
were taking place in 1870 after "four silent centuries":

> The face of the hills was now scarred where men had scraped for
> iron-stone. The sides of the hill had been pierced and tunnelled and
> gutted for coal. Blast furnaces, steel works, company shops, brewery
> and public houses, had appeared on the scene. The counties of Gla-
> morgan and Monmouth had become the magnet south into which
> multitudes of men, women and children had been drawn from north
> and mid Wales, and from the west of England. They came from dis-
> tant rural areas on foot and in carts, they came as Christians and pa-
> gans, thrifty and profligate, clean and dirty; and gradually sorted
> themselves out in their new surroundings according to tradition and
> habit...The empty valley was turned into a long trough full of human
> beings bustling and jostling each other for food and drink.[32]

Jones remembers seeing, as a boy in the 1880s, Italians on the
streets who had come to sell plaster statuettes which they balanced
on a board on their heads: but whether they were resident in the
country or itinerants like the German bands he also saw — three or
four sad and miserable wandering performers in blue uniforms — he
does not say.[33] The chances are that the Italians he saw were residents, for the census enumerator's return for Merthyr Tydfil shows
that an Italian figure maker, Louis Galloezzi, his wife and five sons,
were living in Picton Street in 1881.

As the population expanded, demand for houses greatly exceeded
supply, and speculative builders moved in, filling the valleys with
long, dreary streets of ill-built terraced houses. Overcrowding was
rife, with many houses sheltering two, three, or even four lodgers, in
addition to the family. Sanitation was poor and outbreaks of disease
were common.[34] Typhoid, scarlet fever, measles and phthisis,
croup and whooping cough were endemic.[35] But for all that, there
was glamour in the frenzied activity, and a welcome neighbourli-

ness in the overcrowded valleys. For Bert Coombes, a farm-boy in Herefordshire, the distant glare of the blast-furnaces at Dowlais had long beckoned. When he finally left his parents' farm, to work in a Glamorgan coal mine, just before the First World War, he was not disappointed. The village where he lodged was not attractive to the eye, but he surveyed the wider scene with new-found wonder:

> ...grey house crouched tightly to grey house with no relief of colour and no garden or back entrance; and leaves were grey, and never green, and berries were black before they were red. The dread of consumption was among the people like an ever-present shadow.
>
> Yet, away from the dirt of the village one only had to walk a few hundred yards and there was a wonderful valley sheltered by mountains that made me gasp with amazement. Trees covered the lower slopes and showed their darker greenness up to where the mountain grass and brown ferns seemed to meet the sky at the summit...
>
> A first-class road went along the valley and many people were out walking. Groups of girls, dark-eyed and animated, sauntered along arm-in-arm in search of mischief or adventure. The young men were well dressed and keen in appearance...
>
> It was one of the boom periods of the coalfield, and everyone seemed contented and happy.[36]

Other newcomers to the valleys were to share this contentment while it lasted.

From Bardi to Wales

Somehow, the news of this boom time in Wales reached Bardi and first a trickle and then a steady flow of men and boys set out for Wales to enter, of all things, the café trade. Among them were itinerant organ-grinders, farmers, wood-cutters, charcoal-burners, carpenters and cobblers, and young boys with no employment at all. They went in such numbers that, today, most people in Bardi have relatives in Wales.[37] How did this come about, and who went first? It is said that the news came by sea. Wood cut from the hills around Bardi was sent to Cardiff and Swansea to be used as pit props and coal was sent back to Genoa. Through this trade route, the story goes, came news of a land paved with gold.[38]

There is little to support this story. Italy was certainly a large importer of Welsh coal, and Genoa was the main receiving port.

Ships from Wales would be arriving every day. But communication between Genoa and Bardi was very poor, and the Genoese themselves sailed to America while the *Bardigiani*, by long tradition, headed north. The main route out of Bardi led to Lugagnano, Piacenza, and Milan. This was the route the emigrants took in the nineteenth century, and for many the goal was London.[39] Lucio Sponza, in his wide-ranging study of the Italian poor in Britain in the last century,[40] examines in great detail the origins and occupations of the Italian colony in the Holborn district of London, especially the area around Hatton Garden and Saffron Hill. Those from Emilia came from a specific area: the valley of the upper Taro, quite close to Bardi, and from the valley of the Ceno itself. Sponza's examination of passports granted in Bardi in a nine-month period in 1843-44 shows that, of five hundred and thirty-two issued (mostly to peasants and farmers bound for Lombardy), seventy-two went to organ-grinders, of whom twenty-eight gave London as their destination.[41] The enumerators' books for the 1871 census of England and Wales show that there were many Italian itinerant musicians in Holborn in that year, including twenty-two from Bardi in a lodging house at 9 Little Saffron Hill. Although the enumerators' books for the previous census, in 1861, are not so forthcoming about the places of birth, Sponza's analysis of names and ages shows that many of those from Bardi who were in residence in 1871 were already there in 1861.[42]

By 1881, the Italians had spread along the roads in Holborn. My own perusal of the census returns showed that no fewer than fifty-four itinerant musicians (organ-grinders) had taken over part of the premises at 1 & 2 Robin Hood Yard, off Leather Lane, which in 1871 had been occupied by people of British birth. The musicians were all born in Italy, although the exact place of birth is not recorded. However, the surnames of the residents — Antoniazzi, Berni, Bracchi, Conti, Fulgoni, Rabaiotti, Sidoli, Zanelli, and others — leave little doubt that this was a Bardi enclave. The lodging house keeper was Francesco Rabbaiotti (spelt 'Rabbajotti' by the enumerator); he was also the *padrone* (master) of the organ-grinders who are listed as his servants.[43] At the time, organ-grinding in the colony was beginning to decline. It had been the main occupation in 1871, but between then and the end of the century it steadily gave way to ice-cream making and vending.

5. Giuseppe Conti, standing left, is the baby in white in plate 4.
This photograph may have been taken while he worked for Tanzi in Aberystwyth, but the seated man is unidentified.

Sponza shows that during this period London became a source of Italians in search of new 'pitches' elsewhere in Britain, and draws on a collection of reports for 1903 by the Italian Vice-Consul in Cardiff for a statement that one large group of Italians in the consular district consisted of itinerant people, including organ-grinders, and ice-cream and chestnut vendors, who "generally [came] from London".[44] From people such as these, news of the industrial boom in Wales would have filtered back through London to Bardi.

When they were asked, recently, 'who were the first Italians to go to Wales?', the customers of the Piccolo Bar, in Bardi square, had no hesitation in replying. The Bracchis, the Bernis and the Rabaiottis of Grezzo, a village just a few kilometers up the hill from Bardi: they were the first. This is a view widely shared in Bardi and among the Welsh-Italians in Wales.[45] Some are more precise. In a radio programme in 1980, John Massari, whose father journeyed to Wales at the age of twelve to work for the Bracchis in Aberdare, said "Giacomo Bracchi — he was the founder of all these shops, he was the

6. Italians from Grezzo, in Wales c. 1909. *Standing* (l to r): Giovanni Rabaiotti, Giovanni Berni, Francesco Berni, Giovanni Rabaiotti, Giuseppe Rabaiotti, Luigi Bettosi. *Seated* (l to r): Luigi Rabaiotti, Giacomo Bracchi, Antonio Berni, Antonio Rabaiotti, Stefano Basini Gazzi.

pioneer".[40] It is, however, inconceivable that these were the first Italians in Wales, or even the first from Bardi. As we have seen, there were already some two hundred and forty people of Italian birth in Wales in 1871, including many sailors, and no-one suggests that this particular group of *Bardigiani* had arrived as early as that.

If the questioner had asked who were the first from Bardi to enter the catering trade in Wales (and to be fair to those at the Piccolo Bar, this is probably the question they had in mind), there would be some support for the answer given. Plate 6 is a photograph of Italian café owners in Wales, taken in about 1909. All are from Grezzo. Giacomo Bracchi is among them and so are the Bernis and Rabaiottis; but other families are also represented.[47]

A glance at some of these surnames in the Index of Births in the General Register Office, and an examination of a number of birth certificates, provide further, and harder, information on the dates of arrival of these families in Wales. The records show, for example, that the wife of Giacomo Bracchi, Caterina Bracchi (formerly Fulgoni), gave birth to a son, Francesco, in December 1893. The child was born in 124 Commercial Road, Newport, and Giacomo Bracchi is described as a refreshment house keeper at that address. However, he was not there in 1881 — the date of the last census open for public inspection at the time of writing — and there is strong circumstantial evidence to suggest that he was in London at that time. The enumerators' books for the Holborn district list a twenty year old Giacomo Bracchi as one of the itinerant musicians at 1 & 2 Robin Hood Yard. This is the same age as that of the Giacomo Bracchi who went to Wales, according to a note in the *Western Mail* of the latter's death in 1940. The note records that Giacomo Bracchi, pioneer of the ice-cream and confectionary shops in South Wales, and founder of the firm of Bracchi Bros., was in his eightieth year and had been in Britain for more than sixty years. This would make him twenty years of age in 1881 and resident in this country at the time. It is reasonable to assume that he was the organ-grinder in Robin Hood Yard in Holborn.[48] If the assumption is correct, then Giacomo Bracchi must have arrived in Wales sometime between 1881 and 1893. His daughter, Irena, believes that he worked for a time in a colliery at Beaufort in Monmouthshire.

Another of those in the photograph, Giovanni Berni, was married and living in Swansea in 1894. The birth certificate of a daughter,

7. The Bardi-Lugagnano omnibus in the market place at Bardi, 1906. The bus took emigrants down to the railway in the plain on the first stage of their journey to Wales.

Maria Luiza Francesca, born in October of that year, records that Giovanni and his wife, Teresa Berni (formerly Roberts), were living in 5 Ebenezer Street, which the 1881 census shows was the Roberts's family home. At the time of the birth, Giovanni Berni was an ice-cream vendor. His marriage to a Welsh girl was unusual, and his early naturalisation as a British subject in 1910 (like that of Giacomo Bracchi in 1908), was a very rare event.[49]

Giacomo Bracchi was soon to move from Newport to Canon Street, Aberdare, where a daughter, Irena, was born in January 1897. The birth certificate gives Giacamo's occupation as 'confectioner'. The premises at 26 Canon Street are widely thought to be the site of the first Italian café in Wales but Giacomo's sojourn at Newport suggests that this is not correct. Another contending establishment is Louis Berni's temperance bar in Tredegar, an advertisement for which, published in 1939, carried the message that it was founded in 1880.[50] This must be a misprint, for the enumerators' book for the 1881 census shows that these premises were occupied by Thomas Price, grocer, his wife, four sons, two daughters, three shopmen, and two servants, not one of whom was an Italian. In the absence of further evidence, Giacomo Bracchi's establishment in Commercial Road, Newport, appears to have been the first Italian refreshment place in Wales.

The foundation for the Italian catering trade in Wales was therefore laid in the 1890s and consolidated in the following decade. Various Rabaiotti families had cafés in being, and ice-cream carts on the streets, well before 1907, and many of the pioneers, including the Sidoli brothers who arrived in Wales, one after the other, between 1892 and 1907,[51] were actively recruiting local lads in Bardi to help with the expansion of their businesses. Antonio Assirati left Santa Giustina in 1902 at sixteen years of age to seek a better living in Wales, and joined the Bernis at Merthyr Tydfil.[52] Giovanni Conti did the same in 1908.[53] It would, however, be wrong to suggest that all the Italians in the catering trade in Wales came from the Ceno Valley. A few came from small towns and villages just beyond the boundaries: in the area of Bettola, some twelve miles to the north of Bardi, and from Bedonia and Bogataro a similar distance to the south.

What were these businesses like? In his novel, *The Alien Land*, John Parker describes an Italian café in the main thoroughfare of Aberdare. The scene is set in 1902, and the café is owned by 'Giuseppe Marti', a character modelled on Giacomo Bracchi. Although the characters are fictional, the background is based on fact and appears to have been well researched. The café is seen through the eyes of a young boy who has just arrived from Bardi to work in the business:

> Angelo's first impression of it was of a long, low room with a mysterious door of dark glass at the far end. All along one side of the room was a high counter...and in the middle was a big, pot-bellied stove with a proud looking copper kettle steaming contentedly on the top of it. It was a damp, muggy day and the heat from the stove was overpowering, even near the doorway of the shop, but two men were squatting on tilted chairs close to the stove, talking shrilly in strange voices, apparently unaware of the heat.
>
> There were glass shelves behind the counter and arranged upon the shelves were glasses and bottles of various colours and lines of china cups. Below the shelves were boxes containing multi-coloured sweets and alongside them other boxes placed upright to display the packets of cigarettes inside them. Towards the middle of the counter was a

glass case containing cakes, some iced and some filled with cream...
At the far end of the counter, as far away from the over-heated stove as
it was possible to get, was an ice-cream container, a highly-coloured
cabinet with a lid like a French sailor's cap in the middle of it.
The room seemed much bigger to Angelo than it really was and as he
walked across it towards the dark glass door, following the proprietor,
his boots grated on the fine sand covering the stone flags.[54]

Here we have all the ingredients of a classic, early Italian café in
Wales: sweets, cigarettes, hot drinks (mainly tea and Oxo: the
coffee-machine which was to become the hall-mark of the later cafés
had not yet arrived), non-alcoholic cold drinks, some simple snacks,
a warm place where men could linger and talk — and ice-cream.[55]
Whether by design or accident, the Italians had hit on a recipe for
success in the thriving valleys. The local population, crowded in
their mean-built houses, had few civic amenities. Here was a home-
from-home, a social gathering place where there was no obligation
to buy the wares, however long you stayed. The drawback of this for
the owner was that takings were low, but with hard work and careful
cultivation of the customers, the cafés thrived and business grew.

2:

The Rise of Temperance Bars

"The working men, sir, do not take to coffee taverns"

L ittle is known about where the money came from to fund the first Italian cafés in Wales. At a fairly early stage in the development of these cafés, local banks, with money to invest and an eye for business, took a hand. Peter Bracchi's maternal grandfather started his business in Pontadawe in this way, with a bank loan to buy his first horse and cart to sell ice-cream.[1] It is doubtful, however, if the first aspiring café owners had such help. Banks require some evidence that a business is likely to succeed, and that an applicant is someone they can trust: unknown aliens would hardly fit the bill.

It is more likely that the money came from itinerant, or semi-permanent, activities elsewhere, in London or other cities of Europe, particularly Paris. While most people in Bardi were destitute, a few families would have accumulated money in this way. Before the exodus to Wales, Paul Sidoli's great grand-father walked from Bardi to Paris, opened a millinery shop, and eventually walked back, carrying his money in a body belt, for safety.[2] Even the humble organ-grinder in London could build up some savings to take back to Bardi to add to the family pool of money. A *padrone*, who took a large share of all the earnings of his organ-grinders, could in fact become quite prosperous. And when the organ-grinders in London turned to selling ice-cream, they found it a relatively profitable business, at least in a good season.[3] There is evidence that the first Italian shops in Wales were owned by families still in Bardi, rather than by individuals in Wales. One of the Rabaiotti families in Grezzo certainly operated in this way. Brothers would take it in turn, year by year, to manage a shop in Wales, and the profits were shared out back in Bardi. Other shops were then opened using money from this pool, and gradually the brothers took up permanent residence in Wales.[4]

The amount of money required was in fact quite small, even in London. It cost Giovanni Fulgoni £10 to open a fish and chip shop near Praed Street in Paddington, most of that going on a wood-fired range.[5] Premises were generally rented and furnishings were few. A modest ice-cream business could be set up in the back room of a house, and it may be that Giovanni Berni, who lived with the Roberts family in Swansea, started in this way. In Wales, fuel costs for a café stove were low, with coal so close at hand. Slowly and painfully, the business could be built up — a hand-cart now, a horse and cart later — so long as income exceeded the running costs and the profits were ploughed back in. Long hours, hard work, and a frugal life went hand-in-hand with expansion of the business.

By 1900, the sale of ice-cream in the streets in summer was in full swing and the café owners looked to Bardi for boys to push the carts. Thus began the second flow to Wales, as John Massari relates, recalling what his father told him:

> All the boys used to leave, because there was no work there...Giacomo Bracchi used to go to Bardi to the market, and people with young boys would say, "Mr Bracchi, would you like to have my boy to work for you? Take him to England". "All right, 30 shillings a month and I'll give them clothing, feed them and look after them." He used to go over there and bring back about 10 to 15 boys over. In the summer he'd send them out with the ice-cream cart. On Sundays they would work in the shop.[6]

The late Charlie Forlini was one of those who came. When he was nearly ninety, Herbert Williams interviewed him for the radio programme 'The Bracchis of Bardi', and asked him how much he was paid at first:

> Twenty-five lire a month — £1 a month — with food and clothes. The contract was for 30 months...They sent me out for one year with a hand cart; the second year with a horse and cart, selling ice cream — ha'penny cornet or a penny wafer, or a tuppenny for a man with plenty of money — a tuppenny wafer. [In the winter] chips on the street, every

8. Giuseppe Rabaiotti with his ice-cream cart in Phillip Street, Mountain Ash, c. 1907. Giuseppe had to struggle with his very heavy cart up the steep terraces, built in 1859 for Navigation Colliery.

day like a milkman: you come out with a plate, if not, paper. Penny, tuppenny, it all depends.[7]

The complementing of ice-cream in summer with chips in winter was important not only to ensure a steady flow of sales but also, after 1905, to keep the young employees continuously in work, as the newly introduced Aliens Act required. If sales on the streets slackened it was necessary to find alternative employment for them, and one employer, Giacomo Conti of Cwm, near Ebbw Vale, would turn to building work for this purpose. With the coming of 'the pictures', he was also enterprising enough to arrange for his boys to take trays of sweets and ice-cream into the local cinema all year round.[8] The relationship between the café owners and their new employees from Bardi, and the impact of the legislation on the pattern of emigration to Wales, are examined below.

The Aliens Act 1905

At the end of the nineteenth century there was mounting concern in Britain about the effects of immigration. In 1880, a committee of the House of Commons began to look at the "serious increase in the number of destitute aliens" arriving in the country, but its deliberations led nowhere. The subject was next picked up in Parliament in 1896, when it received a mention in the Queen's Speech. Two years later a bill passed successfully through both Houses of Parliament, only to be dropped. In 1902, a Royal Commission under the chairmanship of Lord James made a "full and complete" inquiry, described by its chairman as "two years of patient study". The members of the Commission were divided in their conclusions but a majority report in favour of tighter controls met with the approval of the Government and led to the introduction of an Aliens Act in 1905.

The Bill which preceded the Aliens Act was strongly contested during its passage through both Houses of Parliament. It was argued by the opposition that the premise on which the Bill was based — that low-priced alien labour displaced 'English' labour and increased the pressure of poverty — had not been proven by the James Commission, and that if there was any problem of this kind it was largely confined to Stepney; there was little sign of it elsewhere in London or in other parts of the country. The opponents of the Bill also argued that its main provision — that an immigrant should be considered as undesirable if he could not show that he had in his possession or was in a position to obtain the means of decently supporting himself — discriminated between the rich and the poor, rather than between the respectable and those who might be troublesome. [9]

The Government stuck to its guns. Winding up the debate on the third reading in the House of Lords, the Foreign Secretary (Lord Landsdowne) described the clause as essential to the Bill. It was, he said:

> ...aimed not at mere poverty, but at a kind of destitution which made it evident that the destitute person was unfit to take his place in the community and that if he attempted to do so he would become a charge on the rates, and would inevitably find his way to those collections of miserable people who herded together in parts of London and became a regrettable and dangerous feature of that city. [10]

There is no doubt that the Bill was heavy-handed. Immigration in Britain, while rising, was far lower than emigration by the native population and was unlikely to have a widespread effect upon employment. The Government admitted that its concern was related to immigrants from "Eastern parts of Europe" (i.e. Jews) living in the East End of London, who were people of "low civilisation" according to Lord Balfour. The opposition argued, with some justification, that any local problems that existed could best be dealt with locally, or by other forms of legislation — such as amendment to the laws governing employment in the garment trade — without endangering the freedom of asylum on which Britain prided itself. "Untidyness of dress was no test of moral virtue, and neither was dirt a test of character," said John Downs, passionately, in a speech in the House of Commons. [11] But the opposition argued in vain, and the Bill went through largely unamended.

Throughout the long debate, there was scarcely any mention of Italian immigrants. The trades they practised did not bring them into conflict with the native born population, nor were their numbers high in comparison with those from eastern Europe. Apart from a passing reference to a few rich and lawless Italians in Soho —

whose alleged wealth would ensure that the Act would provide no barrier to the entry of their kind in future — Parliament showed no concern for those already here, or for those who wished to come. The census figures suggest, however, that the new legislation did act as a deterrent to emigration from Italy to England. After rising sharply from about nine thousand in 1891 to nineteen thousand and four hundred in 1901, the number of Italian-born in Britain remained at precisely that level in 1911. While other factors, such as changing conditions in Italy, may have played a part, they are unlikely to have caused such a sharp break in the upward trend.

In Wales, by contrast, the figures continued their steady climb, and this requires some explanation. As we have seen already, at the time the Act came into force the Italian café owners in Wales were expanding their businesses and looking to Bardi for labour. This trend towards a *padrone* system — master and servant housed together — would have been reinforced rather than weakened by the Act. No longer could a penniless person enter the country in the hope of setting up business through his own enterprise. He had to show, at the very least, that he was in a position to support himself, and the simplest way to do this was to obtain guaranteed and secure employment and accommodation in the country before he entered. This a *padrone* could offer on his visit to Bardi: in return he could impose rigid adherence to the terms of employment, and exercise considerable power over the lives of those who worked for him.

The Padrone System in Wales

In looking to Bardi for boy labour, the café owners in Wales were following the old tradition of the organ-grinders. The terms of employment — a fixed contract, with food, clothes, accommodation and the price of a return fare to Italy at the end of a stipulated period of two or three years — were much the same as those imposed throughout the nineteenth century. As early as 1828, a certain Zucconi in Bardi claimed that he was owed money by one Belli, who had taken his (Zucconi's) son to France for organ-grinding. Belli denied that he owed any money and alleged that the boy had been taken not by him, but by some third party who was now in England and out of contact. This man, said Belli, had given money to the boy to pass on to the father. There is no record of the outcome of this dispute but the police suspected Belli, who had engaged in such traffic before.[12]

In 1844, Caterine Rossi of Bardi sought a passport for her thirteen year old son to go to England with a Giovanni Rabaiotti. The authorities took their time to approve this request because the father's permission was required and he was not around. By the time the passport was issued, Rabaiotti had left for London, but someone else was found to take the boy.[13] These cases show that there was an established practice for sending boys abroad from Bardi and it would appear that some form of payment to the parents was involved.

In 1892, when the problems associated with undesirable aliens were being debated in Britain, W. H. Wilkins drew attention to the "disgraceful traffic" in Italian children carried out by the *padroni*:

> The traffic is carried out in this wise: the children are brought over from their natural country by men who obtain them from their parents for a very small sum, for a few ducats annually...
>
> The *padroni*, that is the masters, having obtained the possession of the children, then bring them by circuitous routes to England. How the slavedrivers — for they are little better — manage to evade the new Italian law against their traffic is not easy to say, but when they have got clear of the frontier their course is plain. Some travel by railway, but many of them actually journey by foot, from town to town and village to village, all the way up to Dieppe or Calais, from thence crossing over to our shore.
>
> The *padroni* are cruel and pitiless masters, and treat their children just like slaves. If the little ones do not bring home a sufficient sum they are cruelly beaten and ill-treated, kept without food or nourishment and sent hungry to bed.[14]

Here, Wilkinson is referring to professional *padroni* who relied entirely on the earnings of children and who employed them in what he called the most degrading pursuits — mainly begging. He draws a distinction between "this class of Italian" and those who took some definite trade such as "confectioners, cooks and waiters" who supplied a "felt want".

Most of the Italians in Wales in the period 1900 to 1920 came, as we have seen, to the café and ice-cream trades. The *padroni* were respectable people engaged in a respectable trade and they were well known to the parents of those they employed. They were very different from those described by Wilkins, and far from cruel to the children. Nevertheless, they imposed a stern and often harsh regime. They had themselves worked hard for long hours and had known privation. They had no compunction about imposing similar conditions on their employees. The boys, however, disliked the regime and considered that they were being exploited by their masters. Many, at a very early age, looked forward to the day when they would be free to start their own businesses, and they buckled down, through the long days, to work to achieve this end.

Giuseppe Conti left Porelli, in the parish of Crederola, for Wales in 1910 to work for Tanzi in Aberystwyth. Tanzi had a reputation for being a good employer merely because he allowed his boys time off to go to mass on Sunday. For the rest of the week, however, he drove them hard. Three boys were employed in the business, and there were three ice-cream carts, with different size containers. The first lad up in the morning took the cart with the smallest container, and so had less ice-cream to make by hand and less to sell. It is not difficult to imagine the morning scramble not to be the hindmost.[15]

There were other cunning devices to make the boys work hard. Joseph Opel arrived in Wales from Bardi in 1908 when he was twelve years old. At Dover he was refused entry and was sent back to France, but he was rescued by a Mr Cavaccuti and went to Kenfig Hill to work for the Sidolis. Each day he pushed a handcart from Kenfig Hill to the seaside resort of Porthcawl — about five miles each way. If he sold all the ice-cream he was allowed to return to Kenfig Hill by train with his empty cart, paying the fare from the takings. If there was any ice-cream left, he had to push the cart back and sell what he could on the way.[16]

Italian family ties are strong, and although the boys from Bardi lived-in, and were in some ways treated as members of the family, they took second place, in terms of business, to the owner's blood relatives. In 1902, Antonio Assirati left his parents' smallholding in the parish of Santa Giustina, ten miles from Bardi, to seek his fortune with the Bernis at Merthyr Tydfil. After some years on an ice-cream round he and another lad were put in joint charge of a new Berni shop at Brynmawr, on a profit sharing basis. At first, the takings were very small but gradually, and with much effort, the business improved. When it was doing very well, he took up what he

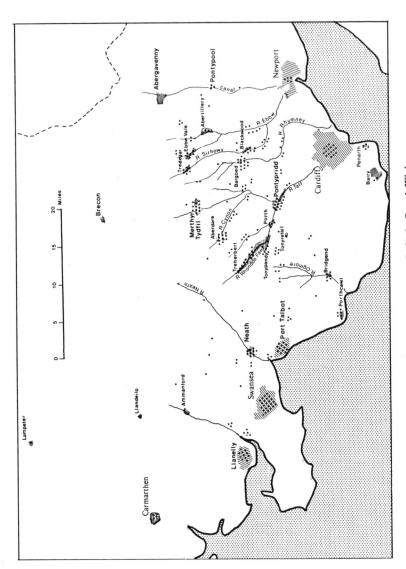

Map 2. The Distribution of Italian Cafés in South Wales

thought to be a kind suggestion by his employers to take a holiday in
Italy and visit his family. When he returned, he found that the
Bernis had put one of their relatives in charge at Brynmawr. He was
given a new Berni shop at Llanbradach, again on a profit sharing
basis, and again he was faced with the task of building up the
business. The whole cycle was repeated, and on his next visit to
Bardi the Llanbradach shop was also given to one of the Berni
family to manage. This was too much for Antonio and he left the
Bernis. He tried a number of jobs before opening his own small
café/confectionary shop in Aberbargoed, which prospered.[17] It
would have been no consolation for him to know that the Bernis
were operating a family-owned business and that those who displaced him at Brynmawr and Llanbradach were probably part-
owners of the enterprise.

Given such conditions, it is not surprising that these young men
sought to get away at the end of their contracts. This was not always
easy even when they had saved enough money, and found suitable
premises, for a business of their own. The more unscrupulous of
their employers did not flinch from buying the property or lease to
thwart their ambitions and stifle competition. In the long run, this
proved a losing battle; the Italian has a strong, in-built urge to be his
own master and the young men from Bardi were no exception. Soon
the cafés were proliferating. In the nineteen twenties there was
scarcely a village in the valleys of South Wales which did not have its
own Italian café. In a small town there was likely to be three, four or
even five, sometimes in one street, and the numbers continued to
grow until the Second World War.

The distribution of Italian cafés, restaurants and fish shops in
South Wales in 1938 is shown in the map opposite. Each dot
represents the approximate location of an establishment listed in
Guida Generale Degli Italiani in Gran Britagna, published in London in 1939. Although the guide identifies many of the Italian
householders in Britain at the time, and gives their occupations, it is
far from complete: some names are missing, and sometimes the
name and address is given without any description of the business.
Thus the number of cafés, restaurants and fish shops in Wales listed
in the guide — about three hundred in all — is less than the number
that actually existed. The map suffers from the same deficiency, but
it does give a reasonably accurate picture of the general distribution

of these establishments. It shows how the cafés were spread along the mining valleys and in the coastal towns, with small clusters in the seaside resorts, but very few indeed in rural areas. Newport, known as the 'graveyard of Italians' because of the number of establishments that failed to prosper there, is an exception to the general pattern. It had very few Italian cafés for its size.[18] It should be noted that to the southwest, the map does not extend much beyond Carmarthen and does not show a scattering of cafés in Tenby and seaside places beyond.

The Immigration of Women.

We have identified two waves of immigrants from Bardi associated with the catering trade in Wales: first came a few pioneers in the 1890s, then young boys in greater numbers about a decade later. There was a third wave, of newly married women, which started to build up slowly between 1901 and 1921.

A few girls had already arrived with the second wave to work as domestic servants to established Italian families. Les Servini's mother, for example, came when she was only thirteen years of age.[19] The numbers, however, were small: in 1901, Italian-born men in Wales outnumbered Italian-born women by nearly eight to one. But as the young boys of the second wave reached the age of marriage, they looked mainly to Bardi for their brides. In the first two decades of this century, the number of Italian-born women in Wales rose from one hundred and twenty-five to four hundred twenty-eight, and the male to female ratio fell from eight to one to less than three to one.

Giovanni Conti, who had left the Bernis for his own café in Blaina, married his third cousin, Maria (also a Conti), while on holiday in Bardi in 1922. They spent their honeymoon with friends in Switzerland and Paris, on the way to Blaina. The twenty year old bride could speak no English, and was not prepared for the wintry weather she encountered during her first summer in Wales. She was taken to the fair, which should have been a profitable day for ice-cream sales, a few days after her arrival. "It was July and they said there was a big fair, but it rained and rained, and I thought 'but, John, it is winter.' But then I got used to it." And with the help of a dictionary and a regular supply of *Christian Weekly*, she soon mastered the English language.[20]

Ernesto Cordani came from Assirati — a group of two or three houses in the parish of Casanova — in about 1902, when he was fourteen years of age, to work first in Maesteg, and then for the Gambarinis in Rhymney. He returned to the Ceno Valley in 1924 to marry Pierina Davighi from Poggiolo, a village only a couple of miles from Assirati and in the same parish. Pierina thought she was going to a land of milk and honey, but her abiding memories of her first days in Rhymney are of pouring rain and gasworks. She also recalls the strange sight of women in 'Dai' caps and shawls, the shining door-steps of the Welsh houses, and the generosity of one of the locals in lending her a mac as she arrived, to keep her dry. Mrs Gambarini, the shop owner's wife, spoke hardly any English, and never ventured behind the counter for fear of being laughed at. She advised Mrs Cordani also to avoid such ridicule, but wiser views prevailed. "Go into the shop," Mrs Cordani was told by an Italian friend, "and speak what English you can. The customers will laugh, and you should laugh with them." And Mrs Cordani, following this advice, soon became accepted. 'Mrs Ernie' she was called by her customers, who readily forgave her for being unable to recognise them in the street as they walked home from work with black faces.[21]

These women had a hard life: preparing food at all hours of the day, serving behind the counter, bringing up children. We look more closely at their family and social life in a later chapter.

The Temperance Bars

As the years went by, the range of Italian catering activities in Wales widened to embrace small confectionary shops at one end of the scale and large restaurants (in the cities) at the other end, with a variety of cafés in between. An analysis of the entries in the *Guida Generale* reveals the following pattern:

Confectioner	4
Café/confectioner	53
Café	187

Café/restaurant	20
Fish restaurant/bar	34
Restaurant	4

As the entries in the *Guida Generale* were probably compiled by the café owners themselves, too much weight should not be given to the figures for individual categories: one man's café may be another man's café/restaurant. There was, however, a noticeable difference between the more ambitious cafés in the market towns and the simpler café/confectionary shops in the smaller villages. The former — which might reasonably be described as café/restaurants — had, by 1939, developed into establishments bearing more resemblance to an English tea room than to the earlier Italian cafés in Wales. They provided cooked lunches and set teas and were frequented as much by women shoppers as by men. Carpanini's 'Square Café' in Blackwood (opposite) was a good example of this trend to cater for a wider range of customers.

The distinction between confectioners and café/confectioners, at the lower end of the scale, was also less clear-cut than the table might imply. With few exceptions, both sold sweets to take away and light refreshmentments for consumption on the premises. In the smaller communities, these establishments retained many of the characteristics of the early Italian cafés, although by the 1930s the fittings had grown more smart and the range of sweets, refreshments, and penny-in-the-slot machines had widened. It is interesting to note that none of the establishments listed in the *Guida Generale* is described as a 'shop' though that was the word most commonly used by the local people in the valleys of west Monmouthshire and east Glamorgan when speaking of a small Italian café — hence my reference, in the Preface, to Conti's 'shop' in Cefn Fforest. Further west, in the Rhondda and Cynon valleys these small establishments were called 'Bracchis' (regardless of the name of the current owner), reflecting the strong presence of the Bracchi families in that part of Wales in the early years of the century.

Here is Walter Haydn Davies's description of a 'shop' in Bedlinog at around the time of the first world war:

> I can still visualise the warmth of the Italian shop in my home village where we congregated as boys round the roaring cast-iron stove with its outlet pipe running through the establishment as if it was a boiler

VITTORIO CARPANINI

The Square, BLACKWOOD,

Telephone 36.   **Mon.**

Luncheons   ::   Teas

Confectionery.   Bakery.   Cooked Meats

High - class   Caterers

9. Advertisement from the *Guida Generale,* 1939

house. Here we gathered to listen to those of our friends who had just started work in the colliery talking 'shop' and presenting us with somewhat idyllic pictures of conditions underground as if they worked in a kind of treasure-yielding King Solomon's mine...

The amount of money spent by these young 'stags' was really very small, a matter of a few pence only, things being so cheap in those days — a packet of cigarettes, for example, could be bought for a penny, a quarter of sweets cost no more, and Five Boys Chocolate Bars were hot favourites at that price. We were the uninitiated schoolboys at this stage, 'orphans of the night' as it were, watching our more affluent companions playing the various games for chits, which would enable them to spend more freely if luck came their way, and then sometimes a few crumbs might come [our] way. 'Flushed' with their winnings the fortunate ones would be likely to stand treat 'all round', in grandiose imitation of the public house routine. In the Italian shop it was not mild and bitter that flowed freely but lime juice and sarsaparilla.

Our Italian only tolerated our presence when things were going well, for he knew that schoolboys more often than not had no money to spend and were merely taking up room. But if anything upset him we were there as a butt for his anger, and with his limited knowledge of the English language he would bawl from across the counter, 'Short boys, out for never!' And we the penniless had to clear out into the cold, to make for some other 'better 'ole', if entry were possible, to a billiard room maybe.

And Davies adds, with respect to this kind of shop generally:

What keen, hard-working businessmen these Italians were! Every possible device to make money was there in those shops and they were prepared to keep open all day and late into the night, indeed, they never seemed to close and even remained open all day on Sunday, to the annoyance and disgust of shopkeepers brought up in the hide-bound Welsh Nonconformist tradition of the puritanical Sabbath day. On Sunday the young men patronised them for supplies of sweets to munch during the chapel service, with reserves for cajoling the young ladies they dated for after-chapel courting sessions.[22]

Contemporary photographs and letter headings show that many of these village shops called themselves 'Temperance Bars'. The three establishments shown in plates 10, 11 and 12 all proudly bear this message on the shop front. This was a development almost unique to Wales, although a few Italian establishments in the northeast of England also bore the name. To see why the name was particularly apt in Wales it is necessary to look at developments in the temperance movement, and in the application of the Sunday trading laws, at the time when these businesses were being established.

The Temperance Movement

In 1830, the Government, in an attempt to wean the working class away from the evils of gin, abolished the tax on beer. Thereafter, no licence was required for the sale of beer. As a result, beer houses increased in number and drunkeness, if anything, got worse. To combat what they saw as the evil of drink, temperance movements sprang up throughout Britain, some seeing total abstinence from all forms of intoxicating drinks as the "true remedy for drunkeness", others preaching moderation. These societies took a number of forms, but common to them all was the signing of a 'pledge', either to abstain or to practise moderation. Some teetotallers, noting that Friendly, or Benefit Societies, often held their meetings ·in public-houses where the members were open to temptation, formed Benefit Societies of their own in more appropriate premises. First and foremost of these was the Independent Order of Rechabites which was formed in Salford in 1835. Others began to encourage children and young people to take the pledge and from this was born the 'Band of Hope' in 1847, which was closely associated with Methodist chapels. Another large society, which was particularly active in seeking legislative change in drinking laws was the Independent Order of Good Templars, whose work in Wales began with the creation of the 'Cambrian' lodge at Cardiff in 1871.[23]

In Wales, temperance and teetotalism were closely identified with nonconformity. "For the Welsh-speaking, evangelical nonconformist," writes W. R. Lambert in his survey of drink and sobriety in Victorian Wales,[24] "the good life for most of the nineteenth and much of the twentieth century, was largely interpreted in such negative terms as teetotalism and Sunday observance." As the working man's leisure time came mainly on a Sunday, so that drinking was concentrated mostly on that day, the issue of drunkeness in Wales became an issue of the desecration of the Sabbath, and during the 1860s and 1870s pressure grew for the closing of public houses in Wales on Sunday. With the backing of the Welsh Liberals, and

10. One of the Rissi (Ricci) brothers' temperance bars in Nelson, in the 1920s.

even of Gladstone himself, the Sunday Closing (Wales) Act was introduced in 1881. Attempts to include the county of Monmouth in the Act did not succeed until 1921, and from 1881 until that time a regular flow of drinkers crossed the Rhymney river every Sunday.

The working of the Act was reviewed by a Royal Commission in 1889. Witnesses in favour of the Act, mainly clergymen and the police, claimed to have seen marked improvements in the behaviour of working men. This was in spite of the proliferation of bogus clubs in which drink was freely available, and of the lax interpretation of the definition of 'bona fide' travellers who could, under the Act, be served with drink in a public-house on Sunday if they travelled three miles or more. "It has removed a source of temptation for many young people," said the Vicar of St. John's, Cardiff, "especially [those] who promenade the streets on Sunday evenings to a very considerable extent, and who, not finding the public-houses open, have no temptation to go in and drink".[25]

Others however argued that the Act deprived the working man of reasonable recreation on his only day of freedom: apart from places

11. Another Rissi temperance bar in Nelson, in the 1920s.

of worship, without the public-houses he had nowhere else to go. The members of the Commission had some sympathy for this view — though not to the extent of making any major proposals for changes to the Act. Speaking of the Sunday influx of young men into Pontypridd from the upper reaches of the Rhondda Valleys, they said:

> We believe that a large number of those who come are young men who have no homes of their own, and we think it not improbable, considering the life which their work entails upon them, that upon that one day of the week which they regularly spend in the open air, they should be drawn to a common centre by other attractions than the mere search for drink alone. But when gathered together at the common centre, they find no place open for social intercourse, or even for shelter from the weather except the public-house [as 'bona fide' travellers] and once there the temptation to drink to excess is irresistible. We think that the true remedy lies either in providing them with reasonable inducements to remain at home, or with places of resort other than public-houses, places which could in some way or other compete with them.

The Commission did not however underestimate the difficulties:

> We are aware that in making this recommendation, we render our-
> selves liable to the charge of going against the prejudices of some who
> hold strong views as to Sunday recreation in any form. We cannot
> blind ourselves, however, to the fact that the strong Sabbatarian
> feeling not infrequently mentioned to us during the time we were in
> Wales, has lost its hold upon many of the class of whom we are now
> speaking, while it retains strength enough amongst those who alone
> could provide the remedy to hinder them from doing so.[26]

This was the rub. Inevitably there was drunkeness and disrepu-
table behaviour on Sunday before the introduction of the Act. After
all, Saturday was pay-day. The Commission concluded that the
closure of public-houses on Sunday should continue, but it was not
against other forms of entertainment — indeed it was strongly in
favour of them. Nor was the temperance movement against such
alternatives. The strict Sabbatarians however would close every
place, whether it sold intoxicating drink or not. In this, they had the
backing of the Sunday trading laws.

Sunday Trading

> You are the Chief Constable of Swansea? — I am.
> How many shops now open on Sundays? —I should say about fif-
> teen.
> Is that because they find they can pay their 5s. and go on? — The Act
> has been the means of closing all the very small shops [in Swansea].
> The small refreshment shops which merely sell ice cream and sweets
> and so forth have taken out refreshment licences to avoid the Act.
> Some of the people own three or four shops; they can only be fined for
> one offence under the Act.
> So that it is worth while to pay the 5s. and open again? — They come
> in every time, bring the money into Court, hand it in, and walk out
> again.

Thus spoke the Chief Constable of Swansea in giving evidence to
the Parliamentary Select Committee on Sunday Trading in 1906.[27]
The Sunday trading law then, as now, was in a mess. The main Act,
dating back to Charles II, was the Lord's Day Observance Act of
1677. It forbade "any tradesman, artificer, workman, labourer or
other person" from "doing or exercising on Sunday any worldly

labour, business, or work of his ordinary calling, works of necessity or charity only excepted."

The Committee found that of the total number of recent prosecutions under the Act in England and Wales, 78 per cent were in Hull, 10 per cent in Swansea and a mere 12 per cent in the rest of the country. It would appear from the Chief Constable's evidence that the high percentage of prosecutions in Swansea was more the result of a vigorous application of the law than of a greater than normal incidence of abuse in the town. After the issue of warning letters by the Corporation, and a large number of prosecutions intended to enforce the Act, the number of shops open in Swansea on a Sunday fell from two hundred and eighty-two in 1900 to the figure of fifteen mentioned by the Chief Constable in 1906. Hull apart, prosecutions elsewhere were relatively few. In Blackpool, to take one example, the police turned a blind eye to the many small shops open on a Sunday provided that they kept a low profile, with no goods on display outside and no doors left open. "It has not tended to create any jealousy or feeling of competition amongst the better class tradespeople, who close their shops and do not mind the little shops being open at all," the Chief Constable of Blackpool told the Committee. He added that he was quite content to see things remain as they were.[28] This is a sentiment with which the Chief Constable of Swansea would not have agreed: he was seeking larger, more effective, fines for breaches of the Act.

The latter's reference to a Refreshment House Licences Act, under which a licence could be issued giving exemption from some provisions of the main Act, took the Committee by surprise. "Can anybody go and ask for it?" they asked. "I think so," was the reply. "...a great many of the shops originally open were ice-cream shops kept by foreigners who, when we put this law in force, took out refreshment licences." He pointed out to the Committee that under the terms of the licence anything bought on a Sunday had to be consumed immediately on the premises; otherwise the proprietor could be fined. This ruled out, of course, the sale of tobacco (and even sweets, unless eaten on the spot) on which the Italian shops so heavily relied.

It is not surprising that confusion reigned and that prosecutions were haphazard, and often brought at the whim of the Sabbatarians. Coffee 'taverns' established in Swansea and the surrounding areas

12. Luigi Conti's twin establishments in Aberfan in the early 1930s. There were billiard tables in the back room.

in the 1880s, to promote temperance, remained, for the most part, closed on Sundays (although they could have taken out refreshment licences) because of uncertainty about the law and opposition from the Sabbatarians. In 1889, the Royal Commission on Welsh Sunday Closing asked Canon Richards of Swansea if these taverns were not acceptable alternatives to public-houses. "The working men, sir, do not take to coffee taverns," he replied dismissively.[29] Even if this had been true of the coffee taverns of the time with their 'do-good' image, the more welcoming Italian temperance bars of later years were to prove the Canon wrong.

The Italians and Sunday Closing

Italians in Wales do not seem to have played any active part in the temperance movement or in the deliberations over Sunday trading. Certainly, none appeared as witnesses before the Royal Commission on Sunday Closing.[30] The shops were called 'Temperance Bars' not because the owners held strong views about intoxicating liquor but from a desire to suggest the convivial atmosphere of a public-house while offering a haven to which parents could let their children go, safe in the knowledge that they would not come into contact with alcoholic drinks. The Italians were not alone in presenting such an image: coffee 'taverns' throughout Britain and the "temperance public houses"[31] which sprang up in London in the 1880s also used the language of the licensed trade to attract their customers; and in 1910, in Pandy Square in Tonypandy, John J Reinecke, 'Botanical Specialist' opened "a new and up-to-date Temperance Bar" with temperance drinks at 1d a glass.[32] For the Italians in nonconformist Wales the creation of a temperance image for their establishments was nothing more than a shrewd commercial move, which caught the chapel-goers in two minds. True, the temperance bars were open on the Sabbath and sold sweets to children on that day, setting them on a downward path; but they also competed with public-houses throughout the week and with the bogus drinking clubs on Sunday. Faced with this dilemma, most people turned a blind eye, and many used the services on offer. Only those with strong beliefs in the proper observance of the Sabbath were moved to bring a prosecution, and their action was sporadic. Nothing on the scale of that in Swansea in the early nineteen hundreds was ever seen again, and as the years went by the nonconformist grip on the industrial parts of Wales weakened. Meanwhile, the café owners paid the fines reluctantly, and carried on.

Louis Massari was one who suffered for a time from the attention of the chapel deacons, and frequently paid the five shillings fine. He became so annoyed with repeated prosecutions that he sent a friend to find if any of the deacons made purchases on Sunday. He learnt that one had a newspaper delivered and "something that looked like beer" from the wine stores. Armed with this information, Louis Massari won the day, and the deacons never bothered him again.[33]

Giovanni Fulgoni's Express Café in Pontypridd had an easier time in later years. The chapel across the road sometimes complained about the café being open on Sunday, but only when the men outside were noisy. They objected much more strongly to trading on Good Friday, but that was only once a year and therefore no real threat to trade.[34]

Sunday trading was essential to the profitability of the cafés as the next chapter will show. There we examine in greater detail the working and social life of a number of cafés in Pontypridd and the Rhondda Valleys.

3:
Pontypridd and the Rhondda Valleys

"See you at Bracchi's"

In previous chapters we have ranged widely over the early history of the Italian community in South Wales and the development of the café trade in coastal towns and in the Valleys. Here, we narrow the focus to look more closely at Pontypridd and the valleys of the Rhondda Fawr and Rhondda Fach, in order to examine in detail the working and social life of some of the café owners. The Rhondda lends itself to such a study. First, it is the largest and most homogeneous urban area in the Valleys, with a well documented history; secondly, its development from a rural to an urban environment was concentrated in the last decades of the nineteenth century and its population was still growing vigorously at the time when the first wave of immigrants arrived from Bardi. The consequent high demand for new services led to the introduction of Italian cafés throughout the conurbation, led by Angelo Bracchi from Bardi.

Pontypridd

Although there was early industrial development at Pontypridd, its importance as a market town owes more to its physical location at the junction of the Rivers Taff and Rhondda than to any growth of local industry. Here the ground is relatively open and, in contrast to the ribbon development of the steep-sided Rhondda valleys, the town had room to expand.[1] This capacity for expansion, and its location on the Taff Valley Railway running north to Merthyr and south to Cardiff, made Pontypridd an ideal site for a regional centre in mid-Glamorgan. It does not, however, seem to have been regarded as a place of beauty, even in its more prosperous days. "Pontypridd is not an earthly paradise", wrote a *Western Mail* columnist in 1904. "It has not the elegant boulevards of Paris, nor the beauteous avenues of some of our English cities. A Cardiff lady took her little daughter to the capital of the Rhondda the other day...and the child was obviously much impressed by the dingy streets and general unattractiveness of the town. After much cogitation in her childish mind, she asked her mother, 'Mamma, is this one of the places where the wicked people are sent to live?' "[2] But whatever it lacked in beauty, Pontypridd made up in its attractiveness to commerce. It drew in the crowds on market days.[3] It was good enough for Giovanni Fulgoni.

* * * * *

On Monday 25 June 1894, *The Times* newspaper reported two dramatic events that had occurred during the weekend. The first was an "appalling and inexplicable crime" which had "convulsed the political world in France": the stabbing to death of President Sadi Carnot on the Sunday, when he was leaving the Palais de Commerce in Lyons, on his way to the theatre. The second was described as "one of the most appalling disasters ever known in the South Wales coalfield:" an explosion at the Albion colliery, near Pontypridd, at 4pm on the Saturday, in which some two hundred and eighty men had been engulfed in smoke and flame below ground, and most were feared lost.

In the following days it became clear that the assassin who had lain in wait for President Carnot among a crowd of applauding spectators, before stabbing him through the heart as he sat in his carriage, was an Italian, Cesaro Santo, born in Motta Visconti in the province of Milan. Santo was an avowed anarchist, with views of the "wildest and most extravagant character", who worked in a bakery in Vienne, just south of Lyons. Fearing a backlash against the many Italian immigrants in France, King Umberto of Italy immediately telegraphed the French Government: "The execrable act which has deprived France of a Chief Magistrate surrounded by universal respect and sympathy has struck me to the heart. The day [the anniversary of Solferino] hitherto sacred to the two nations by a common glory now unites them in common grief".[4] The message failed to achieve the intended effect. Feelings against Italian immigrants in France were never far below the surface, and there had been pitched battles between Frenchmen and Italians in the salt works at Aigues-Mortes only a year before.[5] That feeling now errupted again into violence.

In Lyons, itself, Italian cafés were looted by a mob which continued to maintain a threatening presence outside the premises. Elsewhere in France, those thought to be Italian — organ-grinders, street-cleaners and other labourers — were pursued along the streets until they sought police protection, and Italian businesses were attacked. In Marseilles, a town with a large immigrant population, the mayor urged the citizens not to pursue innocent Italians for the sake of one criminal, but to stay quiet. But the disturbances went on, and other manifestations of anti-Italian feeling began to emerge all over France. Italians employed on extending the college building at St Cyr were dismissed "in deference to the feeling of other workmen" and house-building contractors at Versaille were told by their clients not to employ Italian labour. In just three days, from Lyons alone, three thousand Italians left their homes, many deprived by mobs of everything they possessed.[6] The same was happening in other parts of France, and many Italians sought refuge across the border in Turin.

Among those who left France for Italy was Marco Fulgoni, a building foreman in Nancy, who returned to his home village of Vischeto, near Grezzo, in the Ceno Valley. His son, Giovanni, born in Italy in 1879 but French speaking, did not stay long in the valley. Within a year, at the age of sixteen, he left to find work, first in London and then in Wales, in a number of different occupations, including a spell on the surface at Six Bells colliery, near Abertillery, in the years before 1900. In 1903, he returned to Italy to marry Maria Strinati, also from a village near Grezzo. Later in the same year, he opened a fish and chip shop in Bell Street, off the Edgeware Road in London. A son born in 1904 died shortly after birth. One daughter, Maria, was born in Italy, and two, Vittoria and Ida, were born in Bell Street. In 1915, they moved to Wales, having heard that

13. Interior of the Express Café, Taff St., Pontypridd, c.1916, with mock marble soda fountain in the background. Giovanni Fulgoni, the café owner, is to the right; his wife, Maria, and two daughters, Maria and Ida, to the left.

one of the Basini-Gazzis family had a shop to sell in Taff Street, Pontypridd. Giovanni bought the business but rented the premises. In fact, rent was paid for the next seventy years, until the café closed, as the owners of the freehold would not sell. The fittings however came with the business: a mahogany counter with a bare top, mahogany shelves behind it, and mirrors all along the wall. There was also a magnificent mock-marble soda fountain with a separate tap for each flavour of cordial and a supply of soda water made in the basement using bottled gas. Over the years the Express Café, as it was called, underwent little change. Giovanni's son, Marco, born in Pontypridd in 1918, finally closed its doors in 1986, as leisure habits had changed, and he was reaching retiring age. As the local newspaper put it: 'Express runs out of steam'.

As with other Italian cafés in Wales, the early trade was in soft-drinks, cups of Oxo or Bovril, and ice-cream. The customers were mostly men. Up until the Second World War, the shop was open every day of the year until eleven p.m., although on Christmas day it shut its doors for a few hours at lunchtime. The best days for trading were the market days, Wednesday and Saturday, when people flocked into the town. On Sunday evenings, business was also brisk as young people walked the thoroughfare on the 'monkey parade'. As trade expanded, Giovanni opened other shops — in Abercynon and Merthyr — with managers in charge, but the shops were not a commercial success and they were later sold.

The ice-cream sold at the Express Café was made on the premises from fresh ingredients. In the early days it was produced in a hand-operated machine which consisted of a large wooden tub with a central cylinder (the freezer) around which was packed a mixture of ice and salt. The ingredients were placed inside the freezer and stirred vigorously with a handle until the ice-cream formed. This was then scooped out and finally scraped from inside the freezer. This was hard work, especially when three or four gallons were being made at one time. Relief from this labour came in the early 'twenties with the introduction of a motor drive, followed by electrical refrigeration. The Fulgoni's Frigidaire purchased in 1931 was, according to Marco, the first for miles around. The windows of the café were dressed, free of charge, by representatives of the cigarette and chocolate manufacturers.

The whole family was involved in the running of the business, and their whole life revolved around it. Maria Fulgoni still appeared in the shop, with her own stool, when she was ninety-eight years old. Ida worked there for the full seventy years of ownership. Marco started young, took over the business when his father retired in 1952, and ran it until the end in 1986. As with other Italian cafés, customers could stay as long as they wished and spend as little as they liked. One courting couple used the café as a meeting place and sat before the fire for three hours each evening, day in and day out, for twenty years. During the three hours they bought one pork pie between them, using two plates and two knives, and two cups of tea. Eventually they married and went to the café no more, but they are still remembered with affection. In the long pit strike of 1926, the miners spent even less, but the shop somehow survived.[7]

The Fulgonis did not lack Italian neighbours. In Taff Street alone there were at least five Italian cafés in the 1930s: Servini at No. 29, Franchi at No. 41, Fulgoni at No. 68, Pinchiaroli at No. 93 and

14. The Italian School, Pontypridd, c. 1931

Antoniazzi (number unknown); and there were at least seven others in nearby streets: Conti, Cordani, Marenghi (two), Orsi, and Rabaiotti (two).[8] But with the hours worked, there was little time for social gatherings. Pinchiaroli, for example, kept his café open until the last bus arrived from Ferndale at 11.50 p.m. in the hope that someone might buy a cup of coffee; it was open again at 6 a.m. the following morning, unless it was a Sunday. Then there were fewer workmen around and the cafés did not open until 9 a.m.[9] The Cordanis were also noted for keeping very late hours.

For the Fulgoni family, recreation was a luxury. Giovanni went to Cardiff on Thursday afternoons to play cards and talk to other Italians, and Maria went once a week to see a cousin — one of the Gazzis — at Ferndale. The family also took it in turn to visit Bardi once every three years. There was little else until the 1930s when, once a year, an 'Italian outing' took place, either to the country (Tintern Abbey seems to have been a favoured place) or to the seaside. These were sponsored by the Italian consulate in Cardiff, ostensibly to foster a feeling of pride in being Italian.

Ida and Marco went to the local school and mixed with local children out of school. Marco had much the same recreational interests as the local boys — a love of sport, particularly rugby and football, and later of dancing. He attended an 'Italian school', also sponsored by the Consulate, which met twice a week in the local school building where the children were taught the Italian language. Plate 14 is a photograph of the 'school' taken in about 1931. Marco Fulgoni can be seen standing between and behind the two seated men in the second row, the one on the right being Capt. Sineo, the Italian Consul from Cardiff.

Ida and Marco both married into Italian families, Ida marrying Domenico Pini, who was living at Oakengates, near Shrewsbury, and Marco marrying Luisa, a second generation Welsh-Italian girl from Llanelli. Marco's two children, who both attended the local Grammar school, have turned away from the café trade and have entered the professions. Anna-Maria won a scholarship to Atlantic College and subsequently took a degree in Law at Southampton University. She is now an international lawyer in Milan. John graduated in accountancy at Nottingham University, worked as an accountant for a short while, and then went back to study at Yale, where he took a Master's degree in Administration. He is now a

15. Italian School in the Rhondda, complete with the Italian flag and some Welsh pit winding gear in the background.

16. A Welsh-Italian outing to Jersey Marine, Swansea, in the 1930s.

senior accountant in the United States.[10]

The Rhondda

'The Rhondda' is the name given to two valleys lying to the north-west of Pontypridd: the Rhondda Fawr and the Rhondda Fach. In the early 1800s, these were remote and sparsely populated valleys. Even as late as 1851, the population density of the parish of Ystrady-fodwg, which embraced most of what is now the Rhondda, was less than one person for every twenty-four acres. In the following decades all this was to change. Beneath the moorland and the underlying sandstone ran seams of high quality bituminous and steam coals that were to make the Rhondda famous throughout the world. Some of the upper, bituminous seams which outcropped in the Lower Rhondda, towards Pontypridd, were already being worked by the middle of the century, but the deeper, more valuable steam coal was scarcely being tapped. In 1864, the total coal output from the Rhondda Fawr was less than half a million tons, of which over 70 per cent was bituminous.

The fame of Welsh steam coal was however spreading, and in the next twenty years to 1884 the deep, rich, steam coal measures in the Rhondda were vigorously attacked. Demand was high, prices were good, the technology for deep-mining had been developed; and the speculators moved in. After 1884, few new shafts were sunk but through consolidation of companies, deeper sinkings, and greater mechanisation, the output of coal continued to increase — from 5.6 million tons in 1884 to 9.6 million tons in 1913. The first few years of the present century were in fact the high point of mining prosperity in the Rhondda valleys. In 1913 there were fifty-three large collieries in the Rhondda, of which twenty-one employed more than 1,000 men underground.[11]

In 1919, Dr Morris, of Treorchy, pastor of Noddfa Welsh Baptist chapel, looked back at fifty years of ministry in the Rhondda:

> When I came here in May 1869, the population of Treorchy and the neighbouring village of Cwmparc was 1,200 as compared with about 18,000 at the present day. The population of the Rhondda was 16,814; today it is something like 180,000. Fifty years ago there were seven

Baptist churches in the district with 700 members; last year that number had increased to 52 churches with a membership of 12,000...There were very few collieries here in 1869. There were the Dinas, Abergorky, and Tylacoch pits and those at Cwmparc (Parc and Dare) were in course of being sunk. The nearest railway station was at Ystrad...The Rhondda and Swansea Bay Railway had not come to Treherbert then, and when I wanted to leave the valley for the north or west I had to walk over the mountain to Nantymoel on one side or to Aberdare on the other. As the years rolled on new pits were sunk and new houses sprang up like mushrooms, until the district ultimately became the thickly-populated industrial hive it is today. The hillsides of the valley were thickly wooded in 1869, and the narrow road traversing its length was bordered with hedges and overhanging trees and bushes, and dwelling places were very few.[12]

Tracing the exact population growth in this period is not an easy task, as E. D. Lewis discovered when writing his book *The Rhondda Valleys*. Rapid urbanisation, shifting registration boundaries, and changes in the presentation of census returns, combine to trap the unwary. However, Lewis's own analysis for the years 1871 to 1911 cross-checks well with the published census data. Using this, and data from the 1931 census report for subsequent years, the following picture emerges:

Population of the Rhondda Valleys, 1871-1931

1871	1881	1891	1901	1911	1921	1931
23,950	55,632	88,351	113,735	152,781	166,600	141,790

In terms of rate of growth, the most striking feature of these figures is the doubling of the population in less than ten years from 1871. The population continued to rise in subsequent years, rapidly at first, and then more slowly, until it reached its peak in 1921. The rapid growth in the 1870s was achieved by a rush of people from the valleys around, and from neighbouring Welsh counties. In the following decades the immigrants came from further afield: from the rest of rural Wales and from England, particularly the counties of the south-west. There was also an influx from Scotland and Ireland and from a number of European countries.[13] There was only one Italian-born person in the Rhondda in 1881 (a female), fifty-nine in 1901 (female), and one hundred and seventy-three (thirty-six female) in 1911. Only two had become naturalised British subjects by 1911.[14]

After 1921, the total population declined quite sharply as people left the troubled coalfield in the 1920s. The 1931 census returns show that the rate of outward migration from the Rhondda in that decade was higher than that of any other place of any size in England and Wales. The boom was over. As Gwyn Thomas put it with mordant wit, hundreds of gravestones in Trealow cemetary bore the inscription: "Not dead, gone to Slough".[15]

Tonypandy

Although the Rhondda is an almost continuous ribbon development, certain townships can be identified, among them Tonypandy in the Rhondda Fawr. It was here, at No 5, De Winton Street, that Angelo Bracchi, from Bardi, established the first Italian café in the Rhondda in the early 1890s.[16] Mr T. S. Jenkins can still remember the café as it was from 1912 onwards:

> It affected our lives then, and still does. The café, just below the Square at Tonypandy, was quite an important place... From being a sweet and ice-cream shop it was converted into a café as well, by the new owners from Italy, Mr and Mrs Bracchi who brought the working staff with them. They were of the superior Italian class — very smart and good looking. They soon saw the possibilities in a cafe where people could meet, have refreshments and a chat after shopping. Then they bought the adjoining premises and fitted it out as a restaurant. They also had a good sized ice-cream plant in the rear [which] supplied the valley cafés as well. They engaged attractive young local girls to serve and run the café and the hours of business were extended to the evenings. That brought in the young who were delighted to have such a meeting place especially during the darker seasons of the year. "See you at Bracchi's", was a popular cry.
>
> Mr and Mrs Bracchi stayed there for a number of years. When they went back to Italy as they grew older, younger Italians took over and kept up the good work. ...[It is] still very popular with the general public. It has nice rooms (with central heating these days) and the back room is quite private — very clean and well decorated with pictures of Italy... The Italians are now part and parcel of the life of the valley, and are very popular.[17]

The prosperity of the café, and of the others that sprang up in

Tonypandy, was tied in to the prosperity of the nearby coalmines. Closest were those owned by the New Naval Collieries Company: Pandy Colliery (opened in 1875-9) and Anthony Colliery (1910) in Tonypandy; and Ely (1880) and Nantgwyn (1892) in Penygraig. In 1908 (when the concern became part of the Cambrian combine) these pits employed between them 2,640 men. Not far away from the square at Tonypandy — barely five hundred yards — were the 'Glamorgan' collieries of the Glamorgan Coal Company at Llwynypia which, between them, produced half as much coal again as the Naval collieries and employed more than four thousand men.[18] This company was also part of the giant Cambrian Combine, a powerful association of companies formed around the nucleus of the Cambrian Collieries in Clydach Vale to control the supply of coal and hence its price. On change of shift, many thousands of men from the Glamorgan and Naval collieries moved through the streets in and around Tonypandy in the early 1900s. Many went into the temperance bars for a cup of tea and a smoke, and some even left their packets of cigarettes on a shelf behind the counter to be picked up at the end of shift.[19] In 1910, however, these cosy arrangements were rudely interrupted.

In the period 1869 to 1914, miners wages were linked to the selling price of coal — on a direct sliding scale up to 1903, and by various agreements later. With a fluctuating export market, and fierce competition between the coal producing companies, the earning potential of a miner was subject to sharp and unpredictable change.[20] Although the combined income of a Rhondda family was not inconsiderable in the first decade of the twentieth century, these fluctations, often exacerbated by local conditions, created hostility between the workforce and the coal-owners. In 1910, the workers' failure to extract additional payment for work in difficult conditions in a fault-ridden seam at Penygraig led to bitterness, frustration and anger. Following a lock-out at the Ely pit, and a breakdown in negotiations, the twelve thousand men in the Combine collieries came out on strike on 1 November.[21]

On Monday 7 November 1910, with pickets posted at street corners and at entrances to collieries of the Combine, men and women paraded through the streets of Tonypandy and Penygraig. In the evening a large demonstration by strikers was held outside the gates of the Glamorgan Collieries where, with police protection,

71

officials (and, the strikers believed, blackleg labour) were manning the power station and the pumps. Fierce fighting broke out between the demonstrators and the police which continued until after midnight. The police, though vastly outnumbered, managed to split up the demonstrators, many of whom moved back to the Square at Tonypandy. On Tuesday, at 8pm, rioting began in the highstreets of Tonypandy. In the words of *The Rhondda Leader:*

> By 10 o'clock [in the evening] the town was practically in the hands of the mob. Most of the tradesmen had barricaded their windows, but all of no avail. Some of the shutters in the shops were prised up and the windows literally smashed to atoms. In De Winton Street the strikers dislodged a huge brick pillar attached to a gate.
> ...With the dislodged bricks the strikers proceeded to smash the windows of neighbouring tradesmen. A shop owned by Bracchi Bros. was practically wrecked and looted. The windows up and downstairs were broken, and some of the shop fittings taken out of their sockets. The strikers subsequently looted the shop of everything inside, including pans of ice-cream, sweets, cigarettes etc. The occupiers of the shop are said to have made good their escape by a rush to the back of the premises.[22]

Another Bracchi shop was also damaged and seven other shop owners had their windows ransacked and their stock plundered: one chemist, one draper, two gents' outfitters, two confectioners, and one other refreshment-house keeper. Many other shops also suffered minor damage, mainly in the form of broken windows. "Some of us who live over and at the back of our shops were only too glad to make our escape and leave the shops to the mercy of the crowd", one owner said.

On Wednesday everything was quiet in Tonypandy. Police reinforcements had arrived and a squadron of Hussars detrained at Llwynypia without any trouble. Infantry was moved into Pontypridd and the Home Office reported that the Rhondda was under control.[23] The troops stayed into 1911, the year in which the strike collapsed.

The Tonypandy disturbance was not an isolated event but the first manifestation of the social unrest in South Wales which was to characterise the years from 1910 to 1914.[24] At the time, many considered that the looting and smashing of shops in Tonypandy was the work of a few "half-drunken, irresponsible" youths from outside the district, but this is not borne out by the facts. The riots may not have been pre-planned, but there was a pattern to the events that suggests a deliberate attack upon the social order, triggered by, but independent of, the strike itself. The first shop window to go was that of T. P. Jenkins, a draper who also happened to be a leading Rhondda magistrate. Another prime target was the shop of J. Owen Jones, draper, Chairman of the mid-Rhondda Chamber of Trade, and the owner of many large properties in Tonypandy. These, and others like them, held the levers of power in the social life of Tonypandy.[25] The Italians in the town at that time would hardly have fallen into that category, however, and the attacks on their premises, and on other refreshment houses, are more likely to have been spontaneous, the wageless miners reacting perhaps to outward displays of luxury goods no longer available to them. What is clear is that the general violence, unlike that in France in 1893 and 1894, was not directed at the Italians as such. If relations became strained, the effect was not lasting. As we have seen, the Bracchi shop in De Winton street, to take one example, was a popular place in 1912, and remained so thereafter.[26]

The café is now run by children of Ernesto Melardi who came to Wales from Grezzo a few days after his sixteenth birthday in 1920. Ernesto was the son of desperately poor *mezzadri* who worked land at Grezzo belonging to relatives of Giacomo Bracchi. Through this connection, Ernesto received the patronage of Giacomo Bracchi who brought him to work in his café in Canon Street, Aberdare, after buying him his first pair of new shoes for the journey.[27]

Giacomo Bracchi had five children — three sons (one of whom died young) and two daughters, and at the time of Ernesto Melardi's arrival he owned nine shops in and around Aberdare. Neither of the surviving sons stayed in the business and the domination of the Bracchi's of Grezzo over a large part of the cafe trade in mid Glamorgan came to an end with the second generation. Most of the cafés were sold to other Italians. The name however lived on as all the Italian cafés in the Cynon Valley were called 'Bracchis'. Similarly, Angelo Bracchi's surname became attached to all Italian cafés in the Rhondda.

Giacomo Bracchi and Angelo Bracchi were first or second cousins. In the autumn of 1920, Giacomo Bracchi's elder daughter, Irena, who was born in Aberdare in 1897, married Angelo's son,

Guilio. Irena moved to 5 De Winton Street in Tonypandy, where Guilio had just taken over the business from his father. She took Ernesto Melardi with her. Here he joined another assistant, Jonah Servini, an older and stronger man, who had the strength to push an ice-cream cart up the mountain slopes. His cry, "Make a wafer for a penny, two a penny cornet", could be heard for miles around. Ernesto at first stayed in the shop, scrubbing the floor and polishing the furnishings, and carrying out domestic chores in the Bracchi's quarters. Soon, however, though he spoke little English, he went off to run another shop owned by the Bracchi's in Pentre, further up the Rhondda Fawr, which sold pork pies, ice-cream, sweets and cigarettes. He went there, on and off, throughout the depressed 'twenties and came to love the people of Pentre. They were kind to him when times were hard, even to the extent of providing him with food, realising that the shop was not his, and that he could not afford to eat the wares. Business slackened, too, in De Winton Street especially during the strike of 1926 but the staff — Ernesto, Jonah and two local girls — were kept on, though with reduced wages, and the striking miners were still welcome to sit around the stove even if they had no money. A cigarette was given to anyone who would start a song, and this was handed around as others joined in. The butt was awarded to the one who could sit longest on the hot stove.

In 1929, Ernesto Melardi returned to Bardi and married Maria Bacchetta from Costa Bella, a tiny hamlet close to Bardi. Maria's parents were also poor *mezzadri*. The young couple stayed in a primative building in Grezzo until just after Christmas, when Ernesto returned to Tonypandy leaving Maria with her parents. Ernesto could not afford to go back for three years, but during this time he saved ten shillings a week and this enabled him to buy a house and a piece of land in Grezzo. Their first child, Tina, was born there in 1933, but Ernesto did not see her until she was three years old.

In March 1939, Ernesto brought his wife and child to De Winton Street — a cultural shock for the five-year old Tina who could not understand a word of the language and wanted to go back to her 'granny'. By this time, Guilio was dead (although only in his forties) and buried with his father, Angelo, in the cemetary in Bardi. Ernesto Melardi took steps to buy the café from Irena Bracchi but his plan was thwarted by the outbreak of war, which caught Mrs

Bracchi on holiday in Bardi, where she remained until 1946. During this time, the Melardis ran the business and paid rent into Mrs Bracchi's bank account.

In June 1940, disaster struck. Italy joined the war on the German side, and three policemen, one a sergeant, turned up at the café and arrested Ernesto, who was subsequently interned in the Isle of Man. Mrs Melardi, fourteen months in the country, speaking little English, and eight months pregnant, would have been utterly lost but for her next door neighbours, Mr and Mrs Rogers, who, with help from Ernesto's shop assistant, John Davies, took control and kept the business going. Eight months later, the young Tina went down with diptheria and was placed on the danger list. At this point the local shopkeepers stepped in and petitioned the Home Office for Ernesto's release on the grounds that there was not the slightest possibility that he would carry out any traitorous act. Within a week, Ernesto was back in Tonypandy, firewatching. Although confined to the town he counted himself lucky to be released so early from internment.

After the war, Irena Bracchi returned to Wales and negotiations for the sale of 5 De Winton Street were resumed. The position was complicated because, over the years, many partners had been taken into the business: there were eight of these in all. To simplify procedures Mrs Bracchi bought out the other partners and sold the business as one entity.

Ernesto and Maria had five children in all: Tina, born in Grezzo in 1933; and four born in Tonypandy in the 1940s: Luigi in 1940, Tereza in 1943, Toni in 1945, and Irene in 1948. All went to Tonypandy Catholic School (and Tereza afterwards to a Commercial school) and then into the shop. Tina married an Italian, Pierino Cordani who came from Bardi after the last war; Luigi, Toni and Irene married Welsh people; Tereza is single. All are involved in their own catering businesses. Most of the grandchildren, however, have struck out in other directions — one graduate electronics engineer in Phoenix, one computer programmer in the Civil Service, one hairdresser and one professional footballer. Of those old enough to work, only one is staying in the café trade: Toni Melardi's eldest son is carrying on the tradition, behind the counter in Tonypandy.

Porth

The town of Porth, in Lower Rhondda, sits astride the junction of the Rhondda Fawr and Rhondda Fach rivers, and is the gateway to these valleys. It is the nearest town in the Rhondda to Pontypridd. Its past prosperity was based on coal and fizzy drinks. Two industrial and commercial giants shaped it.

The shallow bituminous coal seams at Hafod and Cymmer — both within three-quarters of a mile of Porth — were among the first to be worked in the Rhondda. These valuable seams were still being exploited in the 1880s when William Thomas Lewis, one of the most influential of all the coalowners in the South Wales coalfield, sank three great pits at Trehafod to the steam-coal seams below, to match, and then exceed, similar developments at Cymmer by Insole and Son. In 1900, these three pits, the Bertie, the Trefor and the Hafod, and the older bituminous pits at Hafod, were welded by Lewis, later Lord Merthyr, into the Lewis Merthyr Collieries Company Limited which, at its height, produced nearly a million tons of coal a year.[28] In 1904, the company also sank the Lady Lewis pit, just north of Porth on the road to Ynyshir, one of the last collieries to be opened in the Rhondda.

Coal was not the only product exported from the Porth area, and the mines were not the only employers. Thomas and Evans's 'Corona' mineral waters, first produced under the name of 'Welsh Hills' at Porth, were, in the 1920s, being delivered to doorsteps in all parts of Britain.

William Evans was born in rural West Wales in 1864. At the age of twelve, he was apprenticed to a grocer in Haverfordwest and subsequently became a junior in William Thomas's grocery stores in Aberbeeg. When he was nineteen, he joined Pegler's Stores as manager of their Porth Branch. Two years later, in 1885, with this experience behind him, he formed a partnership with his former employer, William Thomas, to set up a grocery and provision shop in Hannah Street, the hub of the developing commercial area of Porth. The driving force behind this enterprise was Evans; Thomas was merely a short-term investor who trebled his money in three years, after which the partnership came to an end (though his name continued to be associated with the business). Thanks to Evans's

76

drive, the business had expanded by the mid-1890s to include a bakery in Hannah Street and three branch grocery shops.

In 1897, he took the risky step of cooperating with a "somewhat seedy" uninvited visitor who claimed to know how to make soft drinks. Though the liason was short-lived, Evans was aware of the potential demand for soft drinks as a substitute for alcohol and he pressed on alone. His experiments were to lead to the establishment of the greatest soft drink industry in the world, and the only industry, other than coal, of any size in the Rhondda. With one eye on the temperance movement, and the other on consumers, he chose the right names for his beverages. 'Hop bitters' and 'football stout' sounded fine to the drinkers and were acceptable in coffee taverns and the temperance hotels.

In 1908, *The Rhondda Leader*, praised these "wholesome and delicious" drinks, but the cafés, the corner shops and other potential outlets proved resistent. The Italian cafés produced their own cordials cheaply and were not inclined to change. Others retailers thought it too heavy to carry away. Thus, through necessity rather than desire, the door to door deliveries began. They were a great success, and Evans, and the town of Porth prospered.[29]

In spite of the grim deprivations of the 1920s and 1930s, and the virtual demise of coal mining throughout the Rhondda in more recent times, Porth is still a lively town. There is bustling activity in the Bacchetta café, delicatessen, and restaurant in Station Street on shopping days.

Serafino Bacchetta was born into a poor farming family in Gazzo, near Bardi, in 1899. He was one of six children: five boys and a girl. In 1914 Serafino left his parents, Giovanni and Domenica, and was taken to join two older brothers, Giacomo (John) and Giuseppe (Joe), working in Rabaiotti cafés in Newbridge, Monmouthshire. Another brother, Lorenzo, came to Britain later; but one brother, and the sister never left the Ceno valley. In 1915, John was called back for military service in Italy. He died that year at Cremona, less than forty miles from Bardi. In 1917, three years after his arrival in Newbridge, Serafino was also called up for national service in Italy. He stayed for two and a half years, and then returned to Wales. After a brief spell with Charlie Forlini in Tonyrefail (who had also been with the Rabaiottis in Newbridge), he rejoined Giuseppe and Lorenzo, who had meanwhile moved to nearby Gilfach Goch, to work for the Tambini brothers. Here, in partnership with the Tambinis they ran a shop each, for which they were given a small share of the profits. Giuseppe and Lorenzo also sold ice-cream in the streets but this was not Serafino's scene. He preferred to stay in the shop. "I did not get much," Serafino said later, "about thirty shillings a month". Lorenzo was doing rather better, and in 1932 was able to lend Serafino enough money to purchase from the Rabaiotti brothers a sub-lease on their 'Station Café' at No. 3 Station Street, Porth.

In the previous year, Serafino had married Dorinda Sidoli, who was also living in Gilfach Goch but whose home was in Chiesa Bianca, near Bardi. The second child in a family of seven children, Dorinda, born in 1912, left home at the age of fourteen to go into service in Milan, before leaving for Wales. After the marriage they stayed briefly at Gilfach Goch before Serafino took a partnership in a fish and chip shop in Abercynon at a cost of about £100 in 'key money'. It was here that their first son, Renato (Ron), was born in 1932. The stay in Abercynon was, however, short-lived; later that year, the Bacchettas moved to Porth.

Plate 17 shows the Station Café at Porth as it was at about that time. Rabaiotti accounts for the café in 1928 give the following figures for the turnover in the week beginning 20 May (rounded to the nearest penny):

Sunday.....	£7	15s	9d
Monday......	£6	0s	6d
Tuesday....	£5	3s	6d
Wednesday...	£5	2s	1d
Thursday...	£6	14s	9d
Friday......	£9	8s	4d
Saturday	£11	1s	11d
TOTAL........	£51	6s	10d

The profile is typical for a week in that year, with peak trading at the week-end and a Sunday turnover well in excess of that on mid-week days. It explains why the Italians were keen to keep open on that day. The weekly total varied from month to month, occasionally rising to as much as £80 in the best weeks. Serafino's first entry in the same accounts book in January 1933 shows that he managed to trade at much the same level, with receipts of £64 5s 4d

17. Bacchetta's café, 3 Station Street, Porth, in the early 1930s

18. Station Street, Porth, thirty years later, with Bacchetta's (as now) at nos. 2, 3 & 4

in the first week. Eight years later, he was taking double this figure. The account books show that the café was open every day of the year, except Christmas day.

When the Rabaiotti's five year lease on No. 3 Station Street expired, Serafino took out the next lease himself, direct from the owner, Mr Fudge, and this was renewed from time to time. The rent in 1943 was £65 for the year. In 1957, twenty-five years after moving in, he bought the premises outright, for £200. Later, he bought Nos 2 and 4 as well. Plate 18 shows the premises at Nos 2, 3 and 4 as they are today. There is a café, a delicatessen and a sweet shop downstairs, and a restaurant with waitress service on the first floor.

In February 1936, four months after Mussolini launched the Italian attack on Ethiopia (see Chapter 4), Serafino took out British nationality. Equivocal at first in their response to Mussolini's action, the British Government soon condemned it and British newspapers took a more critical view of Italy than they had before. The ensuing unease amongst Italians in Britain about their position led to a quickening of the pace of naturalisation. Serafino led the way in Porth, and his brothers also followed suit.

In 1937, Mrs Bacchetta gave birth to male twins: Aldo and Mario. A girl, Sandra, was born in 1946. As with other Italian families, the Bacchetta's social life was constrained by the business. Serafino enjoyed an hour playing cards and chatting at the local social club. Dorinda devoted herself to the family and the Catholic church at Ynyshir, and she also took pleasure in cooking traditional Italian meals in the home (there was no call for Italian food in the café) and in dress making. When she died in 1979, simultaneous Masses were held at St Mary Magdalene RC Church at Ynyshir and at her native village church in Chiesa Bianca.

In the 1930s there were a number of Italian families nearby: Camisas and Bertorellis in Hannah Street; Carpaninis in Pontypridd Road and Gambarinis in Tynewydd Square; and as the years went by the number of family connections in Wales and in England increased. Serafino's brothers established their own businesses in Penygraig, married and had children, and many of Mrs Bacchetta's brothers and sisters came to Wales or to London. One worked in the shop in Porth.

The four Bacchetta children attended local schools, at first in

Porth and then the convent school at Clydach, and Ron went on to
Porth Grammar School. The three boys all worked in the business,
Aldo and Mario running for many years a separate café, near the bus
station in Porth, which had been purchased in 1955. This was sold
in 1974 when Mario died and is now a Chinese restaurant. Ron and
Aldo became progressively more involved in the café complex in
Station Street which they took over when Serafino retired and
which they run to this day.

Ron married a Welsh girl of Austrian extraction on her father's
side. Aldo also married a Welsh girl, Mario married a member of the
Bracchi family, and Sandra married a native Italian. She is now
living in Italy. Generally speaking, the third generation of Bacchettas have chosen not to enter the café trade. Among them is a wife of a
doctor living near Rome, a graduate in Business Studies working for
the Burton Group, a graduate in Geomorphology and in Geotech-
tonic Engineering working in consultancy, and a postman. One
granddaughter, however, works in the café, as does the wife of one
of the grandsons.

Serafino Bacchetta died in 1986, aged eighty-six. He was, said
Aldo, "a proud and honest business man. He will be sadly missed by
the Italian and the local community".[30]

Other Valleys

The pattern and style of living we have seen in the Rhondda was
repeated in other valleys of South Wales. The importance of family
life, concentration on successful running of a business, a limited
opportunity for leisure activities, good rapport with the Welsh
people and a continuing contact with Bardi, are all typical of Italian
life in Wales in the first half of this century. The trend for second
generation Italians to attend local schools and then stay in the
business was also a common feature, as was the move into the
professions by their children. The Resteghini family of Blackwood,
and Giovanni Conti's family of Newport, followed this pattern
exactly. Vic Resteghini's daughter (third generation) is a pharmic-
ist, and his son a dentist. John Conti's two sons (also third generation) both went to public schools; one is now a barrister, and one an
engineer. In both families, as with Marco Fulgoni in Pontypridd,

19. Andrea ('Pete') and Vittorio ('Vic') Resteghini with two assistants in their Blackwood café in the 1940s. The display of porcelain barrels and glass sweet jars was typical of many Italian cafés in Wales, including that of Giovanni Conti in nearby Cefn Fforest.

the catering business was sold when the second generation retired.

There are, of course, exceptions, and no two families are exactly alike. In some cases the break with the café trade came earlier. Ino Conti, a second generation Italian from Treharris, became a school teacher; Victor Spinetti from Cwm went into acting, and one of his brothers became a drummer in a well-known group. There are also examples in the other direction: the third generation Carpanini brothers in Mountain Ash both help in their parents' café and run a fish and chip shop next door.

In terms of migration, Giovanni Fulgoni of Pontypridd was outside the main stream in that he set up business first in London and stayed there for many years before going to Wales. But he was not unique. Celeste Resteghini from Chiappa, near Bardi, arrived in London in 1899 and worked as a West End chef until 1923. In that year, a brother-in-law in Wales, Luigi Ricci, persuaded him that there was more money to be made in the Principality than in London and they opened two shops together in Blackwood. 'Ma and Pa' (as the Resteghinis were known by the locals) ran the 'West

End' restaurant, a name that reflected Celeste's time in elegant London restaurants. Blackwood, however, was something of a comedown; even the most affluent customer spent much less in one visit than the average paid for a single vegetable served in London.

In spite of these variations from the general pattern, the Italian community in South Wales, though spread throughout the valleys and the coastal towns was, in the period under review, remarkably homogeneous. [31]

4:
'Enemy' Aliens

'All of a sudden, Les Servini, who was well known
in the town, and whose friends were all Welsh,
was now an enemy alien.'

I n Gwyn Thomas's novel, *The Dark Philosophers*, the central
characters, a group of unemployed, or only casually employed,
'voters' or 'elements' inhabiting the terraces of a mining valley,
retire to the cosy backroom of an Italian café whenever they want a
quiet talk. Although a product of Thomas's fertile imagination, the
café rings true, as does the relationship between the owner and his
patrons. One half-expects to find the café in the *Guida Generale*,
but, of course, it is not there. It is located, presumably, somewhere
in the Rhondda of Thomas's youth:

> Our new meeting place in the evenings was the refreshment and con-
> fectionary shop of Idomeneo Faracci, an Italian, whose shop was on
> the third Terrace, not far from the Library and Institute, where we
> had now taken out fresh membership cards for the sake of attending
> lectures and borrowing books. This Institute was a useful place for all
> voters whose minds liked to dwell on those serious topics with which
> the Terraces slopped over, and there was room there, too, for those
> whose maximum in the way of mental action was billiards, ludo or just
> coming in out of the cold...
> But for the purpose of a quiet talk among ourselves ... we preferred
> the back room at Idomeneo's. This room was cosy and cheerful, hav-
> ing sawdust on the floor and a large stove in the middle, which had a
> complicated system of airshafts that made the lay-out of an ordinary
> man or woman look simple. Idomeneo had never properly mastered
> the ways of this stove, and every now and then thick clouds of smoke
> would come from it and blot out the person to whom you were talk-
> ing...

Besides the stove there were also some tables of various sizes on which the customers could drink hot cordials and eat the sandwiches that Idomeneo served, and we always praised the hot cordials of Idomeneo for being prepared with great skill and great heat. Our own drink was tea and we drank a lot of it. We had taken a vow to get our stomachs as dark as our philosophy before we finished, and every time we ordered a fresh round of cups Idomeneo always put an extra pinch in the pot as a tribute to the fine brooding quality of our spirits...

Idomeneo had an old cabinet gramophone in the back room, and a large bundle of records containing such items as very sweet arias from operas, also duets, trios and choirs, and to these Willie and ourselves would sit and listen by the hour, with Willie bursting out with his own version sometimes if there was a tenor on, and Idomeneo giving him strong support in a baritone voice that seemed to us very deep and rich for so small a man. And when the music had ended and Idomeneo was bringing us our last cup of tea of the night...the only sound in the shop was the roaring of angry, complicated draughts through the twisted shafts of the stove, the beat of Idomeneo's tired fingers on the counter (he opened the shop at six in the morning), rain outside beating down upon the terraces...

Such places as Idomeneo's shop which never seemed to close, were very popular shelters with the voters and [one] night, as we were sitting in the back room waiting for Willie, a large number of these elements, drenched, had crowded into Idomeneo's shop out of the rain... Some of the people, to thank Idomeneo for letting them in out of the rain, bought small bags of sweets such as pennyworths of hard mints or twopennyworths of toffee in paper, which was considered very classy things to eat in the Terraces. But most of the voters just stood there dripping wet and making a great noise.

My friend Ben did not like this...but Idomeneo said his parents had always told him it was wise policy to be friendly with all, whether they bought articles or not because it was a very poor voter who went through life without ever buying anything.[1]

At one point in the story, an emblem on the hot water cistern on the counter of the shop captures the attention of the group:

The cistern had been made in Italy, and just above the name of the manufacturer, which was stamped on a chrome plate, there was engraved a bundle of rods and an axe. My friend Arthur pointed out to Idomeneo that these rods and so on were the trade mark and symbol of the Italian Blackshirts, and no very healthy sign to be showing in a place like the Terraces, where the voters had never failed to show a great respect for democracy and a will to strive for equal justice.

Idomeneo, who was a short, cheerful man with black hair, said he knew all about this symbol and that he liked it no better than we did.

85

Lime, Lemon and Sarsaparilla

He added that even then he had two brothers in Italian jails because
they had happened to be in Italy when they said they did not like this
symbol either. As far as politics went, said Idomeneo in a whisper, he
was with us to the end... He meant that he was for all the common
people, as we were, being of them.

Idomeneo goes on to explain that, because he was ham-fisted, any
attempt on his part to file away the emblem would greatly damage
the cistern, and the Italian in London who had loaned him the
money for the cistern and who was "partial to the party behind the
rods" might then call the loan in and shut him down. The group is
sympathetic:

> From the moment of that explanation onwards we are good friends
> with Idomeneo, particularly after he had told us of those two brothers
> who were in jail. We looked on him after that as being a splended char-
> acter by our standards, and a valuable link between ourselves and all
> those humble brethren on the continent of Europe whose aim, as ours,
> was to cut down on the number of nuisances who flourish on this
> earth.[2]

The Rise of Fascism in Italy

The party "behind the rods" on Idomeneo's cistern was the fascist
party in Italy, which came to power under the leadership of Benito
Mussolini in 1922. In Roman times the *fasces*, a bundle of rods, with
or without an axe, was carried as a symbol of chastisement before a
high magistrate. Mussolini's black-shirted fascists themselves
'went Roman', using terms like 'centurian' in the hierarchy and
adopting the *fasces* as their symbol.[3] Once the party had established
itself in Italy, its fingers stretched out to reach places where Italians
lived abroad, even touching Wales.[4]

Benito Mussolini, born in 1883 in the region of Emilia, was the
son of a blacksmith of strong socialist convictions, which rubbed off
on the boy.[5] From the start, Mussolini was wilful and quarrelsome,
with a school record of expulsion and suspensions. He did however
survive at one school long enough to take a diploma in 1901. After a
succession of teaching jobs, in which he failed, and short spells of
wandering in Switzerland, he took up journalism, editing in succession the socialist newspaper *Avanti!* and his own creation, *Il Popolo*

86

d'Italia, a newspaper ostensibly socialist, but partly funded by industrialists.

Using this paper as a platform, Mussolini, having broken with the socialists, launched the Fascist Party in 1919. In the elections later that year, the fascists were defeated overwhelmingly by the socialists who, in the number of votes gained, outnumbered them by forty to one. Demoralised, the fascist movement almost came to an end, but Mussolini soon recovered and proceeded to trim his sails to the current winds. Fascism became all things for all men; there was room in the movement for people of all political persuasions, or none. He had learned from his journalism that the public was easily deceived, and without blinking an eye he could appeal at one and the same time to "aristocrats and democrats, revolutionaries and reactionaries, proletarians and anti-proletarians, pacifists and anti-pacifists". Fascism, carefully undefined, was presented as patriotic nationalism; those who opposed it were savagely attacked.

In the elections of 1921, with Italy in a state of political turmoil, thirty-five fascist deputies were elected, including Mussolini. By entering parliament, Mussolini gained immediate immunity from arrest for the violence he had unleashed in his bid for power. Recognising that they could flout the government with impunity, the fascists built up a quasi-military organisation of armed groups. In 1922 they started an insurrection in Milan and threatened a march on Rome. The king was advised to declare a state of emergency; at first he agreed, but then he changed his mind. Fearing the prime minister's ability to control events he asked Mussolini to form a government. Three years after launching his party, and with a tiny minority of deputies in the Chamber, and virtually no representation at all in the upper house, Mussolini became prime minister of Italy. He was thirty-nine years old.

Il Duce

In 1924, Mussolini called an election to consolidate his position. Again, the fascists engaged in a reign of terror, beating up opponents and rigging the ballots. They won 65 per cent of the vote and Mussolini moved quickly towards personal dictatorship, demoting the cabinet of ministers to a consultative role and abolishing the party congress. He promulgated the legend of an all-seeing, all-wise *Duce*. Photographs of him in his best Napoleonic poses appeared everywhere and school teachers were ordered to praise his "wonderful courage and brilliant mind". At the same time, opposition to the regime was being eliminated, the press, radio and cinema subjugated, and entry to many professions restricted to those who could show a good fascist record. The State ruled supreme and Mussolini's strength and popularity continued to rise into the 1930s.

On the face of it, it seems surprising that Italians should have been taken in by such a vainglorious and dangerous man but many were pleased to see the socialists destroyed and the squabbling liberal factions put to flight. Here, at last, was stability. Besides, Mussolini gave them what they wanted — *Dopolavoro* ('after work') clubs with bars, billiard halls, libraries and sportsgrounds for the adult masses, and summer holidays and charabanc trips for children. These were fun rather than propaganda but they were very effective in promoting Mussolini. For the middle classes, there were more jobs in the civil service (which doubled in size in the 1930s), more prestige and more power.[6] Fascism also lavished large sums on the projection of its image in such a way as to appeal to a wide cross-section of the population, appearing sometimes in the guise of extreme socialism and at other times exhibiting unbridled nationalism.[7]

However, much of the support from the masses stemmed more from resignation than from enthusiasm. Even Party members were not always of fascist persuasion; they carried the card out of sheer necessity. "The average Fascist takes no active interest at all in party life," a former secretary of the British Chamber of Commerce in Naples told the Foreign Office later, "[he] views the meetings to which he is summoned as a nuisance, to be evaded or got rid of as quickly as possible."[8]

Fascism and the Emigrants

Mussolini was more interested in building up the male population in Italy to satisfy his military ambitions than he was in the economic benefits of emigration, and he made the emigration regulations more bureaucratic to stem the flow. This, combined with a cut-back in immigration in the United States, and the slackening employment possibilities in other countries, profoundly changed the Italian way of life. Emigration declined from six hundred thousand a year immediately before the First World War to less than fifty thousand in the late 1930s.[9]

As in Italy, Mussolini strove to win over the Italian population abroad. 'Emigrants' became 'Italians abroad', young people "with a mission to civilise the world".[10] C. Cavalli, who was resident in London during the 1930s, wrote afterwards: "the Italian emigrants overseas were more protected and respected, and held in greater consideration than now — 25 years after the end of fascism". Cavalli, though he claims never to have been a "really committed" fascist, joined the party in 1935, enrolling in the London Section:

> Several years before I joined, fascism had taken root in London and a large number of my fellow countrymen living there, including the best people in the [Italian] colony had joined the Party. Others, even if they had not enrolled, were obviously sympathisers. Moreover, most Italians abroad had good reason to be grateful to the fascist government. Before fascism, all Italian governments had taken very little care — or none at all — of the thousands who had emigrated: now things had changed. The fascist government genuinely helped fellow countrymen who had emigrated overseas and as far as possible promoted their well-being.
>
> Thanks to the fascist government some ten evening schools had opened in London alone for the children of emigrants who had been born in London so that they could learn our mother tongue.[11]

Here, Cavalli is underplaying the political side of these benefactions. Although they were given a 'caring' image, and were presented in patriotic terms, they were clearly intended to win support for Mussolini. Similar phrases were used to describe the part-time classes in Italian which had opened in Wales under the sponsorship of the Italian Consulate in Cardiff, and the annual outings to the sea and countryside. If some were won over to fascism by these events, others saw them as a way of building national pride. As in Italy, the outings were seen as fun, and the schools as a welcome cultural development. Indeed, despite the occasional presence of the Consul — who could have been regarded more as a helping Government official than as a party activist — some who took advantage of these measures may not have been fully aware of the political aims behind them, or may not have cared. At these gatherings the Italian flag, rather than a fascist emblem, was likely to be the main symbol on display.[12]

There were however more overt demonstrations, at least in London. To quote Cavalli again:

> The fascist group in London...among whom a strong group of Tuscans were prominent, were united with a single aim: to spread fascism throughout London and the United Kingdom. Following a programme which they had devised themselves, the London fascists often organised balls, receptions with various patriotic displays, at which the fascist emblems were more and more evident...
>
> In the various lectures on fascism which were given in London, the greatness of Italy was praised often and with sincere enthusiasm. The Italians in London, whether fascist or not, had never shown so much enthusiasm for the mother-country as at that time.[13]

The driving force behind all this was the Italian Ambassador in London, 'Count' Dino Grandi. He was no urbane career diplomat, but a powerful figure in the Italian fascist party, a former provincial boss of a particularly violent element of fascism, and a rival, in Mussolini's eyes, for the leadership.[14] During his time in London, formerly independent trade organisations, such as the Association of Café Proprietors (*Associazione dei Caffettieri*) and the Italian Catering Association, came under fascist control. The membership lists of these organisations must have provided the government in Italy with much valuable information on the whereabouts of Italian immigrants in Britain.[15] All this gives some credence to Gwyn Thomas's picture of a fascist in London breathing down the neck of poor Idomeneo Feracci.

The Invasion of Ethiopia

On 3 October 1935 Italian troops invaded Ethiopia (then called Abyssinia) in East Africa to link the existing colonies of Eritrea and Somalia, and to provide space for settlement. The day before, the people of Italy were summoned into the town squares to hear over loud speakers Mussolini's announcement that war had begun. The government claimed that twenty-seven million people took part in this staged demonstration. The people showed, however, little enthusiasm, except perhaps in the main cities, and there was also little response to a call for volunteers to take part in the fighting.[16] In the opening sequence of the film version of *Christ stopped at Eboli*, the camera pans slowly across the fields, showing peasants bent over their work while Mussolini's voice booms out, unattended.[17]

What did galvanise the Italian people into support for the war was the unanimous condemnation by member countries of the League of Nations which followed its outbreak. Like all good patriots under threat (in this case, of economic sanctions), they rallied to the cause, and a quarter of a million married women donated their wedding rings to help maintain the gold reserves.[18] And when Ethiopia fell in 1936, and the new Italian Empire was announced, Mussolini's standing with the Italian people reached its peak.

The organised gatherings to hear the announcement of war in 1935 were not confined to Italy. Dino Grandi addressed a gathering of about five hundred Italian men and women in the Italian Cooperative Club in Soho timed to coincide with Mussolini's speech in Rome. All those who had been invited to attend were asked "without compulsion" to send a telegram to the Secretary-General of the Fascist movement in Rome giving his name and the organisation to which he belonged so that the authorities in Rome "might be enabled to estimate the strength of the numbers of Italians now in foreign countries".[19] The *Western Mail* reported that the Italian Consulate in West Bute Street, Cardiff also presented "a scene of intense activity". The newspaper wrongly attributed this to "orders received some time ago" by Italians residing in the district to report on the outbreak of hostilities "to receive their instructions relative to returning to Italy".[20] The Italian Consul promptly denied that this was the intention. "The attendance of Italians at the Consulate on Thursday evening was due simply to their wish to express their loyalty to and support of the Italian Government" he said, putting another misleading slant on the proceedings.[21] As the Ambassador in London (and therefore, presumably, the Consul in Cardiff) was speaking of the war as a manifestation of the Italian people's "desire and need" for "peace with justice" there may well have been expressions of support — after all, who would not be in favour of that? As in Italy, an appeal was made to Italians in Britain to pour all the gold that they could give into helping Italy to combat sanctions. According to Cavalli, and the *Guida Generale*, the response was generous from fascist and non-fascist alike.[22] Collections were made in Italian cafés in Wales, but for some in Wales, the Ethiopian war was a turning point of another kind. Against a background of anti-Italian comment in the press, and hints from friendly local police,[23] those who might have been hesitating about taking British nationality threw off their doubts and took the final step.

The Second World War

In 1936, Mussolini sent 'volunteers' to Spain to fight, alongside the Germans, for Franco in the civil war. They lost badly at the battle of Guadalajara against a disparate band of amateurs which included many Italian anti-fascists, and by bombing British shipping in Spanish ports they further alienated Britain. Mussolini hailed it, however, as another victory. He began to play along with Hitler and to speak of a Rome-Berlin Axis. In May 1939 he signed a military pact with Hitler, but when Germany marched into Poland in September, and war broke out in central Europe, Italy remained 'non-belligerent' — a better term, Mussolini thought, than the weak-sounding 'neutral' — and remained so throughout the 'phoney war' of 1939-1940. But by May, it was beginning to look as though Germany would be victorious; there were spoils to be had for Italy, or German gains in the Tyrol to be avoided, and the risk of going in on the German side seemed small. On 10 June 1940, Italy joined the war and was in conflict with Britain and France.[24] Overnight, the Italians in Britain became 'enemy aliens'.

'Intern the Lot'

As Italy moved towards war, the British government reviewed its plans for internment, which had already been invoked for German and Austrian nationals.[25] The Germans and Austrians were for the most part recent arrivals in the country and personal details had been collected on entry. At the outbreak of war with Germany, tribunals were set up to place these enemy aliens in three categories: Category A, those expected to help Germany or hinder the British war effort; Category C, refugees and those who had lived in the country for some time; and an intermediate Category B which gave the tribunals some discretion on the restrictions to be applied.

Those in Category A were to be interned, those in Category B were to have restrictions placed on their movements, and those in Category C would remain at liberty.[26]

The Italians, by contrast, had put down roots many decades before and information about them was scant. MI5, however, had compiled a list of fifteen hundred members of the Fascio in Britain, and they took the view that those who had been only nominal members of the Fascist Party and those who were ardently Fascist, were equally dangerous.[27] The list therefore became a list of 'dangerous Italians'. The plan adopted in May 1940 was to arrest these 'dangerous' characters first and intern or deport them, and to intern other Italians later. But Mussolini's announcement of war on 10 June came at a time when Denmark, Norway, Belgium and Holland had been invaded, France was on the point of collapse, and the British Army, in retreat from Flanders, was fighting with its back to the sea. The threat of invasion of Britain was real and the newspapers carried silhouettes of German troop-carrying aircraft so that they might easily be recognised by the public.[28] The Government took no risk; they interned 'the lot' as quickly as they could.[29] By the middle of June, all men of Italian nationality in Britain between the ages of sixteen and seventy had been interned.[30]

The round up was swift. Within hours of the announcement that Italy and Britain were at war, Ernie Carpanini of the Corner Café in Abercynon, was roused from his sleep by a knocking on the door. He found that a police inspector and a sergeant had come to arrest him. He later described what happened: " 'I am very sorry', the inspector said, and he put his arms around me. He was crying as he picked me up".[31] All over South Wales similar scenes were being enacted. Both the police and the Italians were bemused. Les Servini found it very strange when he was arrested by several policemen whom he knew very well, having lived in Port Talbot for twenty-five years. "All of a sudden, Les Servini, who was well known in the town, and whose friends were all Welsh, was now an enemy alien."[32] Overnight, some one hundred and sixty Italians from Glamorgan alone were placed in detention.[33]

This rough treatment by the government can best be described as a mixture of prudence and panic: if there was no time to sort the sheep from the goats, play safe and take them all away. The keeping of a list of known fascists was also understandable, assuming it was accurate, as formal membership of the Fascio involved an oath of allegience to Mussolini. The xenophobic outburst from some of the Press, on the other hand, was completely inexcusable. *The Daily Mirror* was one of the worst offenders:

> Now every Italian colony in Great Britain and America is a seething cauldron of smoking Italian politics.
>
> Black Fascism. Hot as Hell.
>
> Even the peaceful, law-abiding proprietor of a back-street coffee shop bounces into a fine patriotic frenzy at the sound of Mussolini's name...
>
> We are nicely honeycombed with little cells of potential betrayal.
>
> A storm is brewing in the Mediterranean.
>
> And we, in our droning, silly tolerance are helping it to gather force.[34]

Although, as we have seen, the rounding up of Italians in Wales was generally carried out with sympathy and understanding, some of the xenophobia in the press rubbed off. In Swansea hostile crowds gathered outside Italian shops in the High Street and near the GWR station. Windows were smashed and goods were taken from the premises. Outside Antonio Segedelli's shop in Carmarthen Road the crowd of about two hundred reacted violently when the police tried to arrest one of their number for stealing cigarettes, and police truncheons were drawn. In reporting these events, the *South Wales Evening Post* did not condemn them. It drew attention to the "stab in the back" that Mussolini had delivered, and said that if innocent Italians had suffered in the demonstrations, what else could be expected?[35]

A few lesser incidents occured elsewhere in South Wales. A "drunk and disorderly" Markham collier got behind the counter of an Italian fish and chip shop and demanded that it be closed. "I am in charge," he said.[36] There was an altercation in Cwmparc between four young men and a naturalised Italian father and his British-born son, during which the young men were alleged to have thrown stones, to which the Italians had responded by brandishing the whips carried in their ice cream carts.[37] Mrs Viccari of Tonypandy was moved to place an advertisement in the *Free Press and Rhondda Leader*:

MRS A VICCARI
of the Cosy Corner Café
86 DUNRAVEN STREET TONYPANDY
wishes to inform the public
that she is a
BRITISH SUBJECT
and has a brother now serving
in the British Army and also a
brother now serving in the British Navy[38]

Similar scenes were witnessed throughout Britain. Bottles were thrown and windows broken as anti-Italian feeling erupted into violence in Soho; and demonstrations were reported in Belfast. Edinburgh, Liverpool and Manchester.[39]

This extremism must however be put in perspective. There was much sympathy for the Italian people and, indeed, for the Italian state, for the predicament in which they found themselves. "There is no quarrel between the Italian and the British and French people", Clement Attlee told parliament on 11 June, and *The Times,* in reporting this, added that "Free Italy, the land that Mazzini and Garibaldi liberated from Teuton domination and that took up the struggle against the same enemy in 1915...[has been] dragged in the dust by the sordid and avaricious tyranny to which it has become enslaved".

* * * * *

Having arrested male Italians, the government had to decide what to do with them. The internment camps which had been prepared in many parts of Britain to house Category A and selected Category B Germans and Austrians were full and no plans had been made to care for the large numbers of additional internees — Italians and the remaining Germans and Austrians — arising from the adoption of an 'intern the lot' policy. New camps were hastily prepared, including one at an unfinished council housing estate at Huyton, near Liverpool, and another at the derelict Warth Mills cotton factory at Bury.[40] The Home Office then turned its attention to the Isle of Man which had been used for internment purposes in the First World War, and boarding houses and private houses were requisitioned. The Isle of Man eventually became the prison for a large proportion of the men and women interned in Britain.[41]

During this period of activity, Canada, under pressure from the British Government, and with great reluctance, agreed on 11 June to accept three thousand prisoners of war and four thousand internees, the latter made up of two thousand five hundred 'pro-Nazi' Germans and fifteen hundred 'members of the Italian Fascist Party'. Some days later, Australia also undertook to receive internees.[42]

Shortly after their arrest, hundreds of Italians moved from temporary detention centres, such as the Maindy army barracks at Cardiff, to Warth Mills. Among them was Bert Rabaiotti (now living in Cwmbran), his father and his brother. Several members of the Maruzzi family from Wales were also there; one guarding the camp from outside, the others imprisoned within.[43] In a report written a few weeks after his arrival at the camp, Uberto Limentani, an anti-Fascist refugee from Italy, described the conditions at the camp:

> On the 11th day of my permanence [i.e. internment] I was transferred to Warth Mills Internment Camp, Bury, Lancs. In this camp, I found very deplorable accomodation and insufficient hygienic facilities for the 1800 people who were packed in a very restricted space (no possibility of having a proper wash, the dirt and the grease of an abandoned factory spread all over the place, practically inexistent lavatories). The food...was often insufficient, and the evening meal frequently consisted of some bread, a piece of cheese and a cup of tea.[44]

A delegate of the International Red Cross who visited the camp in July also made a critical report of the camp's dilapidated condition and lack of hygiene.[45] Soon, however, many of the internees were on the move. "We were there about a week", Bert Rabaiotti recalled. "From Bury, they separated all of us into different groups. Some went to Canada; some to Australia; some to the Isle of Man. My father was supposed to have gone to Australia; my brother went to Canada; and I ended up in the Isle of Man."[46]

The Arandora Star

In mid-June, the government policy on the disposal of Italians in this country was in disarray. The Foreign Office favoured the deportation of all Italians (not just those thought to be Fascist) back to Italy on the grounds that many who were sympathetic to Britain would be a thorn in Mussolini's flesh. It also thought such a move would facilitate the repatriation of British citizens from Italy. The Home Office was prepared to go along with this, although it knew that enough shipping to deport an estimated ten thousand Italians would not be available for a considerable time.[47] The War Office and the Security Service would not wait: they wanted to take immediate advantage of the Canadian offer.

In the event, it was the mechanics of removal, rather than matters of high policy, that determined the outcome. At a meeting at the War Office on 15 June, at which the sole Foreign Office representative was heavily outnumbered by the military, the Home Office, and MI5, the army movements branch announced that three ships were available to take seven thousand prisoners of war and internees to Canada. It was agreed that the total would be made up of two thousand six hundred Category A Germans; nineteen hundred prisoners of war; and fifteen hundred 'Fascio' Italians. Three thousand would go on the 'Duchess of Atholl'; two and a half to three thousand on the 'Ettrick; and fifteen hundred on the 'Arandora Star'. MI5 agreed to send at once to the War Office a list of fifteen hundred Italians whose removal they desired, marking "if possible" the names of three hundred and thirty "bad hats".[48] Thus the future of many Italians passed out of the hands of the Home Office and Foreign Office into those of the military authorities. "They [the military] can have no conception of the political considerations involved, nor yet of the psychological effects on foreign public opinion of any error of judgment into which they may slip" the Foreign Secretary said later.[49]

After the meeting on 17 June, events moved swiftly. One ship (it was the 'Duchess of York', not the 'Duchess of Atholl') sailed immediately with about two thousand one hundred Category A Germans and Austrians, and five hundred and thirty prisoners of war on board. The 'Arandora Star' became available to the War

20. The 'Arandora Star'

Office on 19 June, and was scheduled to sail on the 25th. To allow for rail travel to the port of embarkation it was essential that the selection of individuals for deportation should be completed by the 22nd of June. The M15 list however did not reach the camps until the day before, and no more than 24 hours were therefore available to identify those on the list and prepare them for the journey. When the 'Arandora Star' finally sailed from Liverpool on 30 June (five days late) it had seven hundred and seventeen Italians on board and four hundred and seventy-three Germans, one hundred and twenty-three of the latter being merchant seamen captured at sea, the rest supposedly in Category A.[50] In the scramble to get the ship away, mistakes in selection of both Italians and Germans were inevitably made.

Until the outbreak of war, the 'Arandora Star', a modern and luxurious ship of the Blue Star Line, with elegant staterooms and spacious cabins for four hundred or more wealthy passengers — all first class — cruised in pursuit of the sun. In June 1940, under the control of the Ministry of Shipping, its funnels painted grey and with armament fore and aft, she took part in the evacuation of British troops from Narvik in Norway, and of troops and refugees from the Atlantic coast of France. On 27 June she steamed into Liverpool where the three thousand people crowded on board disembarked. Barbed wire barricades were installed on the promenade deck and British soldiers, who were to sail as guards on the voyage to Canada, counted the German and Italian prisoners aboard.[51] Among the soldiers was Ivor Duxbury of the Welsh Guards who was astonished to see among the prisoners one of the Rabaiottis he had known so well in Wales.[52]

The Italians were divided into two contingents, one group going to the lowest deck on the ship, the other to cabins at the highest level. When she sailed from Liverpool in the early hours of 1 July, the 'Arandora Star' was carrying sixteen hundred men, including crew. Although this was much higher than her peacetime complement, the degree of discomfort was not unusual by trooping standards, although the lower deck was crowded. Uberto Limentani shared a cabin on the lower deck with three other Italians and was allowed out for three-quarters of an hour during the day to stretch his legs on the deck.

At 7am on 2 July while steaming 125 miles north-west of Ireland the 'Arandora Star' was struck by a torpedo fired from a German U-boat. Limentani was asleep when the ship was shaken by the blast of the torpedo:

> I got up, advised people to be calm, put on my lifebelt, and went on deck. I tried to get into a lifeboat, but, when it was launched, it was nearly empty, and soon the stream and waves pushed it far. The other lifeboats were already far away. Many people had jumped into the sea and a good deal of them had already died. When I realised (about 20 minutes after the torpedoing) that there was not much time left, I got down calmly into the sea, and swam away from the ship, which was quickly sinking. She had turned on the right side, her bow was submerged, people who were on the decks poured into the sea, and all of a sudden she sank with a terrible noise. The sea was covered with oil, somewhere even blazing with wrecks and pieces of wood...[53]

Limentani managed to reach a crowded lifeboat. Around mid-day they were spotted by a flying boat and a few hours later were rescued by a Canadian destroyer which took them to Greenock, near Glasgow. Limentani was one of the lucky survivors: four hundred and eighty-six Italians and one hundred and seventy-five Germans were lost at sea that day.[54]

News of the sinking of the 'Arandora Star', and the publicity given to the fate of the better-known Italians who had lost their lives, stirred the Foreign Office and the Home Office into action. Lord Halifax, in a letter to Anderson, found it difficult to write "with complete restraint" about "a very bad business", and he urged Anderson to join him in securing the hold up of further shipments of Italians to the Dominions. While he was forming this view however, two more ships sailed: the 'Ettrick' to Canada with "an arbitrary selection of some four hundred Italians" among the internees on board, and the 'Dunera' to Australia. Both departments were shocked to learn that the 'Dunera', which sailed eight days after the sinking of the 'Arandora Star', had two hundred and two Italian survivors of the 'Arandora Star' on board who, in spite of their ordeal, had been bundled by train from Glasgow to Liverpool and then treated very badly as they boarded the 'Dunera'. The decision to re-embark them had been taken by the War Office without consultation. "No doubt [they] regard themselves as covered by previous Cabinet decisions that Italian Fascists should be sent overseas", Anderson wrote in a letter to Halifax on the 19 July. In the same letter he told Halifax that he had now issued orders that no more Italians should be sent overseas without his express concurrence. He added that he proposed to take steps to appoint a small committee to visit the camps where Italians were detained and classify them on a systematic basis.[55]

Forty-nine men born in the Ceno Valley died on the 'Arandora Star', and all but a few came from Wales. A small chapel in the cemetary in Bardi, dedicated to the victims of the 'Arandora Star,' lists their names and these are shown in Appendix 2 together with the places of arrest where known. The surnames of many who died will by now be familiar to the reader of this work and would be recognised by anyone who lives in Wales: Basini, Carpanini, Conti, Moruzzi, Rabaiotti, Ricci and Tambini, to select a few. To the names shown in Appendix 2 two more from Wales can be added: Antonio Castelli from Fleur de Lys in Monmouthshire, and Vittorio Lusardi of Llanharan in Glamorgan. Castelli was born in Bettola and Lusardi in Bedonia, both places being just outside the borders of the Ceno Valley. Their names are recorded separately in the

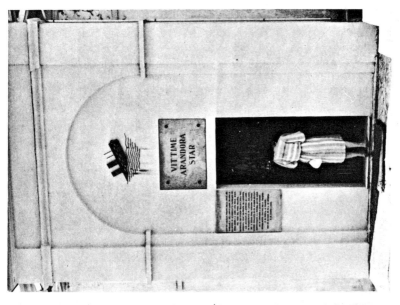

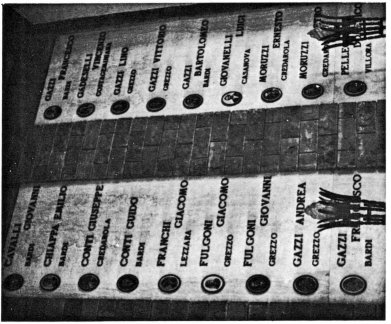

21 & 22. The Arandora Star Chapel in Bardi

23. Welsh Italians in the Tatura internment camp near Melbourne, Australia. *Standing* (l to r): F. Rabaiotti (Pontypridd); G. Gazzi (Ferndale?), G. Lusardi (Bargoed), A. Cavanna (Tredegar), G. Moruzzi (Ebbw Vale), E. Cordani (Rhymney). *Seated* (l to r): L. Fulgoni (Pontypool), G. Rossi (Swansea), G. Lusardi (Ystrad Mynach), G. Foligno (Pontardulais)

chapel at Bardi.

To this day, friends and relatives fail to understand why all these men were chosen for the voyage. "My father should never have been on that boat", said Bert Rabaiotti, in 'Another Valley': "he was never a fascist". Charlie Rossi, in 'Ciao Charlie Rossi', went further. "Not one was a fascist or a sympathiser" he said, "their only crime was that they had not become British citizens".

Some of the survivors from the 'Arandora Star' were also from Wales. Ernesto Cordani, from the parish of Casanova, near Bardi, and from Rhymney, suffered many hardships before reaching Australia. The 'Dunera' was packed with people and the hatches were battened down for most of the voyage. The ship was attacked by a submarine early in the voyage and nearly suffered the same fate as the 'Arandora Star'. The prisoners suffered for two months before the 'Dunera' arrived in Australia. Along with other survivors of the 'Arandora Star', Ernesto was put ashore at Melbourne while the ship went on to Sydney with the remaining men on board. He was taken to a camp of corrugated iron huts near Tatura for internment. Plate 23 shows a group of Welsh Italians in civilian dress in the camp, with Ernesto Cordani on the far right of the back row.[56] The Italians at Tatura were released from internment before the end of the war to work in and around Melbourne, where they had considerable freedom of movement. Some returned to Britain, but others, fearful of the risks involved in a long voyage, preferred to wait for the end of hostilities.

Among the "arbitrary selection" of four hundred or so Italians who sailed to Canada on the 'Ettrick' was Luigi ('Gino') Rabaiotti. After his arrest in Llanelli, he was kept in detention for a few days at Pembroke Dock and then moved to Warth Mills with two brothers, Mario from Swansea, and Bert from Llanelli. These two brothers were taken from the camp to the 'Arandora Star' and Luigi appealed in vain to be allowed to join them. They survived the sinking of the 'Arandora Star' and spent the rest of the war in Australia.

After ten days on a zig-zag voyage, in crowded conditions and with completely inedible food, Luigi disembarked from the 'Ettrick' at Quebec. The Canadians, expecting prisoners of war and "dangerous characters", mounted a strong and heavily armed guard as the passengers were transferred by train to Montreal and thence by bus to St Helen Island camp on the St Lawrence river within sight of Montreal. This too was heavily guarded, and the internees were kept in uniform, but the food was good and plentiful and the Canadians treated them well.

Of the four hundred and seven Italians at the camp, sixty were released after six months having persuaded a British interviewer that they were free from fascist sympathies. The rest, Luigi Rabaiotti among them, were detained until 1943. Then, with the fascist power in Italy in eclipse, he sailed to Britain in the 'Queen Elizabeth' for a further spell of internment, this time in Onchan camp on the Isle of Man. He was released in 1944 for "work of national importance" and ended the war in the employment of the Glamorgan War Agricultural Committee.[57] During the course of the war, his family had been widely dispersed: his sister was in Penygraig, his mother in Bardi, his brother Frank (until the war a wine merchant in Swansea) was in the Italian army in Jugoslavia, and two other brothers, Bert and Mario, were interned in Australia.

* * * * *

In August 1940, the War Cabinet appointed Lord Snell to conduct an inquiry into the method of selection of aliens sent on the 'Arandora Star'. In his report, which was considered by the War Cabinet in November,[58] Snell drew particular attention to the unsatisfactory method of selecting "dangerous characters" from among the Italians, which gave no opportunity for appeal and which was based "mainly" on the basis of membership of the Fascist Party. But he also expressed the view that in the circumstances prevailing at the time there was no alternative. He reached two conclusions. First, that MI5 should bear some responsibility for the deportation of a number of men whose sympathies were wholly with this country. It was a consequence, said Snell, of their decision that nominal members of the fascist party and ardent fascists were equally dangerous. Secondly, that in "about a dozen" cases, the names in the embarkation list did not coincide with those on the MI5 list of party members. Given that the work of selection was carried out under great pressure, Snell did not consider that this number of errors was a cause for serious concern.[59]

Is it possible to reconcile Snell's view that all but a handful of the Italians on the 'Arandora Star' were members of the Fascist Party with the contrary views expressed in Wales by relatives of the Welsh Italian victims? To answer that we have to look at the work of the Home Office Advisory Committee set up after the sinking of the 'Arandora Star', to consider the release of Italian internees on the Isle of Man. Among these were Italians on the MI5 list who, for one reason or another, had not been deported.

Isle of Man

In August 1940, the government published a White Paper (Cmd 6223) giving ground rules for the possible release of civilian internees of foreign nationality. For the Germans and Austrians it was possible to define specific categories for consideration — for example all Category C and some Category B internees who could show hardship, or provide evidence of a public and prominent part in opposition to the Nazi system, or had a British-born son in HM Forces. Similar criteria were to apply to the Italians, but in the absence of any prior classification by tribunals each application for release was to be referred to the Advisory Committee mentioned above.

Sir Percy Loraine, the former British Ambassador in Rome, was appointed to head the Advisory Committee in the Isle of Man. He received an early briefing from the Foreign Office:

> [At] a meeting convened by Lord Swinton last Saturday...it was apparent that our 'security service', i.e. MI5, were firmly fixed to the idea that the Fascist organisation in this country (as distinct from the British Union of Fascists) was a dark and sinister *Camorra* [Italian secret society], that every member thereof was actively engaged in sabotage and 5th column activities and that it was sufficient for them to say that any individual Italian was a member to justify his detention to the end of the war. Under cross-examination, however, they admitted that they were largely influenced in their attitude by fear of invasion. They also admitted that in the majority of cases they have practically no evidence of subversive activities beyond mere membership of the Fascio.[60]

Loraine's own experiences in interviewing Italians in the Isle of Man soon showed the flaw in MI5's reasoning, as he explained in a letter to the Foreign office in November:

> The difficulty is that there is no established definition of [party]

membership. Such of us as are acquainted with Italian conditions, and our knowledge on this subject has been confirmed and developed, in my case at least by having heared over two hundred cases, realise that a man who belonged *in the pre-Fascist era* to an Italian benevolent, social or sporting club, of which the Fascist authority ultimately obtained control, is only technically, indeed barely technically, a member of the Fascio.[61]

This is the key. Snell seems to have been in no position to challenge the validity of the MI5 list; still less could he determine whether, if it was a valid list, those on it were witting or unwitting members of the fascist party. He merely compared the names on the 'Arandora Star' embarkation list with those on the MI5 list and found few discrepancies. His report has been described as a 'whitewash', but 'superficial' might be a better description. He did at least point the finger at MI5 for their insistence that all fascists were equally dangerous.

It would be surprising if Snell got the number of discrepancies exactly right: Italian names being what they are, those responsible for making the selection at the camps would have been very fortunate indeed to get it right within about a dozen. There were three G Fulgonis on the 'Arandora Star' — two of them Giovannis — and there were probably many more of that name remaining in the camps. It is difficult enough to sort out Italian names at leisure; it is almost impossible to do it for more than seven hundred in twenty-four hours.

It is quite possible that some Italians in Wales were members of the Fascist party by default. As we have seen, the Fascio in Britain took over a number of trade organisations in which Welsh Italians were involved, and they even took control of the Italian Legion — the equivalent of our British Legion — which provided social amenities to veterans of the First World War. It is unlikely that many would have withdrawn from these useful organisations, even if they knew that by staying they would technically become members of the Fascist party. In such circumstances, their families could well say that they were not 'fascist'. However some Italians in Wales will have taken a positive decision to join, for the same reason that people joined in Italy — because it offered some economic advantage, for example better assistance from the Italian Consulate in Cardiff over land or property interests in Bardi. And it cannot be said that there were no ardent fascists in Wales. Black shirts were not entirely absent from the streets in the 1930s, though their activities were minimal, and mainly social; and some young men and selected children from the Italian schools went off to Italy, to fascist camps and rallies. They were for the most part responding to Mussolini's call for 'patriotic nationalism'. A meeting of local fascists in Newport in 1936, and another in the New Continental Restaurant in Cardiff, were reinforced by fascists in full uniform from London. Their presence in the New Continental drew a sharp protest from the Labour politician, Leo Abse.

It is however inconceivable that the small café owners in Wales, many of them resident in the country for decades, and with their roots sunk deep, would have engaged in any desperate deeds of sabotage or treachery — of say blowing up the collieries or docks had the Germans invaded. Whatever the technical point about membership of the Fascist party, and whatever fascist sympathies may have been displayed, there was never any real threat. The internment and deportation of these largely innocent people, was a sad episode in British history.

In spite of Loraine's sympathetic approach to his task, there was no immediate flood of releases of Italians from the Isle of Man, more a steady trickle. Loraine could only advise, and the security services remained in a powerful position to influence the final decision which rested with the Home Office. Most of the Italian internees were still imprisoned on the island when, in September 1943, Italy signed an armistice with the Allies. By then, Anglo-American armies were moving up Italy, Mussolini had been deposed as prime minister, and later arrested, and the Nazis were moving in to control the central and northern provinces. Ironically, the man who brought about Mussolini's downfall was Dino Grandi, the former ambassador in London, who had done so much to promote the cause of fascism in Britain. It was Grandi who proposed to the Grand Council in July that the king should be asked to resume some of the powers of which fascism had deprived him.[62] In September 1943, in a daring raid, German commandos released Mussolini from his mountain prison. He was installed as the head of a puppet government in the north, thus plunging Italy into civil war.

As the war in Europe drew to its close, and the last Italian internees in the Isle of Man were returning to their homes and cafés, Mussolini's dwindling band of supporters in Italy deserted him. On

28 April 1945, he was executed by communist irregulars near the Swiss border.[63] Mussolini was then sixty-one. One of Idomeneo Faracci's 'nuisances' had ceased to flourish on this earth.

5:
Today and Yesterday

'Chinese Take Away Open Soon'

The Post-war Period

During the Second World War, and in the decades that followed, the economy in South Wales recovered from the low points of the 1920s and 30s. Although steel and coal output fell at the outbreak of war with the disappearance of export markets, the construction of new factories for armaments and other provisions of war raised the level of employment. In the post-war years, light industry replaced the ordnance factories, the government invested heavily in coal and steel, and a number of government services were moved to Wales. Steel enjoyed a boom that lasted through the 'sixties. The output of coal also climbed until the mid-1950s, but then started its rapid decline.[1]

Although this revival in fortunes was concentrated in the towns rather than the valleys, it brought to the Italian cafés a period of high prosperity. With more money to spend on leisure activities, and with meagre food rations at home, people turned to the cafés and to the fish and chip shops in greater numbers than ever before. We saw in Chapter 3 that Serafino Bacchetta's takings in 1941 were twice as high as they were in 1933. The Italian fish and chip shops — or at least those shops which had survived the shock of internment or deportation of their owners — did particularly well during the war, and were often packed to the doors with customers. This was the heyday of the Italian café trade in Wales.

As the years went by, habits changed. Car ownership, the spread

24. Massari's café is shanghaied—Cross Keys, 1986

of television, the introduction of live entertainment into the drinking clubs, the popularity, for a while at least, of Bingo, and a higher degree of commuting between home and workplace, all served to reduce the appeal of the traditional Italian cafés. Evening trade, in particular, fell away sharply. In the valleys, the consolidation of some collieries, and the closure of others, gained momentum in the 1950s and accelerated rapidly through the succeeding decades. The transfer of miners to places of work away from their old communities robbed those communities of their vitality,[2] and the once throbbing Italian cafés, and the miners' welfare halls alike, saw their clients drift away. Many cafés have been sold to developers; some, like Massari's café in Cross Keys, have been taken over by the Chinese. In Ebbw Vale, before the war, there were six Italian cafés; now there are only two or three. Tony Viazzani, who has one of the few remaining cafés in Merthyr, has given a roll-call for that town: Rossi's Express Café — "closed"; Bracchi— "he's gone"; Dimambro's Queen's Café and Zannelli's — "gone". Viazzani believed that in five years, ten at most, there would be no Italian cafés in the valleys.[3] This is perhaps pessimistic. Some, are still in good shape, although it is what they have on offer, rather than the social life, that pulls the customers in. But the marked fall in numbers is real enough, and is bound to continue: the cafés grew with the boom in coal, and like coal they have dwindled away.

It is impossible to estimate with any precision the number of people of Bardi origin in Wales today. There are no statistics of people who are, say, three parts Italian, one part Welsh, or the other way round, nor even of people of pure Italian blood whose grand-parents or great grandparents came to Wales nearly a century ago: to the census takers they are an indistinguishable part of the native population. One estimate by the Italian Embassy in London puts the figure at around seven thousand,[4] and that is, perhaps, not too far wrong given that there were just under fifteen hundred people of Italian birth in Wales in 1931 (most of them from Bardi) and that two or more generations have gone by since then.

Like others after the war, the *Bardigiani* in Wales enjoyed an improved quality of life. Long days in the café, with just one day's outing a year to the seaside or the country for relief, were things of the past. Longer holidays and shorter working hours gave more time for leisure activities. Dances and other social events were organised to foster a community spirit, and in recent years an *Associazione Amici Val Ceno, Galles* (friends in Wales of the Ceno Valley) has been formed, with its own gazette and a regular monthly programme of social gatherings.

The acquisition of cars and better road and rail communications have made Bardi much more accessible than in the pre-war days and more than ever it has become a 'Little Wales' in Italy. A mini-bus runs regularly between Wales and Bardi in the summer months. Derelict family homes have been restored for summer residence and new villas have been built for the more affluent. Since 1982, there has been, each year, an organised 'festival of the emigrants' with a barbecue and music and dancing in the square. The population rises sharply for this summer peak event and South Wales' accents fill the air.

But behind all this lies a certain unease, a question, if not a problem, of identity. When asked if they felt they were Italian or Welsh, those taking part in the two television programmes about the Italians in Wales gave, not surprisingly, different replies. Some,

111

even among the younger generations, thought of themselves mainly as Italian; their upbringing, family ties and close links with the Ceno Valley, made them so. Others felt more at home in Wales and regarded themselves as predominantly Welsh, but with a nostalgic love of Italy. Any attempt to classify members of the community into these two categories would, however, be unrewarding. The Italians in Wales are the products of two cultures which cannot be untwined, and many accept the advantages of both. As Iolando Rossi put it: "When I leave Bardi I cry; when I leave Ebbw Vale I cry".[5] Or, as a Mancunian Jew said recently in another context, "I am 100 per cent Mancunian and 100 per cent Jew".[6]

But there is an aspect of this duality which rankles with many of the *Bardigiani* : whatever they think themselves, and whether they like it or not, the Welsh regard them as Italians, and the Italians regard them as Welsh or English. Even those of the older generations who have retired to Bardi complain that the natives do not see them as 'belonging' to the town. They are viewed as people who have been 'abroad', and 'picked up money with a shovel'.[7] Indeed, those with a second home in Bardi pay higher rates and taxes than the native population, and this too marks them out as different.[8] This lack of total acceptance is the price the exile pays for any prosperity he has found abroad.

The Emigrants and Bardi

We saw in Chapter 1 that economic conditions were responsible for the high level of emigration from Italy at the close of the nineteenth century and in the early years of the twentieth, and that Bardi was no exception. The peasants were escaping from a wretched life of poverty, and even of starvation, and they were looking for a better life. It is true that in the 1920s and 1930s some anti-fascists left for political reasons, but by then the main exodus was over, and none of them seems to have gone to Wales. The Italian government encouraged the earlier migration though it did little to look after the emigrants after they had left the country. Their only interest was in remittances from abroad which relieved some of the economic pressures and helped with the balance of payment for overseas trade.

In Bardi, conditions did indeed improve for those who stayed behind. Apart from the direct aid provided to families by those who had gone away, there was another largely unforseen benefit. At first, the older generations worked any land owned by the absentees, either to provide for themselves as family, or for a rent as *mezzadre* . As the older generation passed away, the younger generation showed little interest in working the land for half the yield and would only do it on a 'pay the rates and taxes' basis, which amounted to next to nothing in the mountainous area in which the land lay. The absent owner of the land had little choice but to accept what was in fact a peppercorn rent, and was often glad just to have the ground cleared. If he sold the land, the tenant could drive a hard bargain and buy it for a small sum, and often recoup his outlay by felling a few trees.[9]

As plots merged, and roads and water and electricity came to Bardi, the value of the land, and the income from it, rose. Those who had been lucky enough to buy the land cheap reaped the benefits of these developments. The emigrants' loss was their gain.

However, while there were economic gains, emigration was not without its darker side for those who stayed behind in Bardi. The Italian, more particularly the peasant in a remote town or village, has a strong sense of loyalty to his immediate family. The departure of husbands and brothers and sons weakened, or broke, these ties and in some villages destroyed a way of life. More than seventy years after the event, Giovanni Conti still thought of his parting from his widowed mother: "She didn't like it, she didn't want me to go," he told Herbert Williams in 1980, "but, poor old lady, I left [for Wales] and worked for the Bernis."[10]

Today, the wheel has turned full circle. There is little employment for those who are growing up; there is no industry in the Ceno Valley and few people are now required on the land. In winter the town and village streets are empty. The children are leaving. Their prospects lie elsewhere: in Turin and Milan; in France and in Germany. And much as the Welsh Italians enjoy their visits in summer, very few stay on a permanent basis.

The Immigrants and Wales

In 1930 the total population of the *comune* of Bardi was just over six and a half thousand, mostly living in scattered villages and houses.[11] There were at this time about fifteen hundred *Bardigiani* living in Wales. In terms of the size of Bardi, the rate of emigration over the previous thirty years can reasonably be described as a flood. But relative to the size of Wales, which had a population of more than two million at that time, mostly concentrated in Glamorganshire and Monmouthshire, it was no more than a drop in the ocean, despite the fact that Glamorgan had at one time a greater number of Italians in its population than any other county in England and Wales except London and one other. Consequently, the Italian immigrants on arrival in Wales did not face the prejudice and contempt shown to their compatriots who landed by the boat-load in the United States of America. It took the Italians in America many years to shake off the stigma of being 'a Dago' or 'a Greaseball' and the perception of them as illiterate, unskilled, slum-dwellers remained long after the great majority had become middle class.[12]

The assimilation of the Italians in South Wales was eased by the expanding, cosmopolitan nature of the Welsh community. In 1911, for example, Glamorgan had the lowest proportion of native born inhabitants in the whole of England and Wales: only 51.5 per cent of males and 61.2 per cent of females were born in the county.[13] With a large influx from neighbouring areas, from the counties of Cardigan, Somerset, Gloucester, Devon, Hereford, Wiltshire, and from London and Ireland, the population was fluid. Fifty or so immigrants a year from Italy posed no problems of absorption. The nature of the trade they adopted also led to their being well dispersed throughout the native population. The degree of concentration which could occur, even in the main street of a market town, was limited by the need for a café to have a reasonable catchment area from which to draw its custom. In Wales there was, in consequence, no 'Little Italy' as there was in Clerkenwell in London and Ancoats in Manchester. The 'community' was in fact little more than a loosely-knit group of people with common background and common interests. Their geographical distribution militated against any collective endeavours: there was was no Italian hospital, no Italian school building, no Italian church. They shared the facilities provided locally for the rest of the population.

With the native Welsh as customers and as neighbours, it is not surprising that many friendships formed between both young and old. In 1919, fourteen years old Giuseppe Spinetti, newly arrived from Ronchi, was befriended by a local boy who accompanied him on his ice-cream rounds in Cwm, near Ebbw Vale, and acted as interpreter. Giuseppe later married the boy's sister.[14] The young boy with the ice-cream cart shown in Plate 8, also received some friendly help when pushing his cart up the steep hills of Mountain Ash, although here there was the prospect of a free ice cream to act as an incentive.[15] More permanently, Antonio Assirati and his family formed strong bonds of friendship with a family of bakers, the Reeds, whom he first met at Llanbradach and later had for neighbours in Commercial Street in Aberbargoed. When Mrs Assirati died, a few years ago, one of the Reed family who had been an 'unofficial' ice cream taster at the back of the shop in his youth was moved to write that "part of old Aberbargoed had gone".[16]

The Italians were not, however, entirely free from acts of persecution. Giovanni Conti's ice-cream cart had stones thrown at it on ocassion; catcalls about 'b****y Eye-ties' followed others in the streets or playgrounds; and another Conti's ice cream cart was overturned and the ice-cream stolen at a fair in Aberfan in the 1920s. To add to his misery, the icecream seller was stuffed into his cart and wheeled around the ground by local 'lads'.[17] These, however, were the acts of hooligans and children and they seem to have been rare events. In general, newcomers from Bardi were more likely to suffer from the hardships imposed upon them by their Italian employers than from any hostile or unfriendly acts by the native population.

In his study of the Italian poor in Britain in the nineteenth century, Lucio Sponza points to their adaptability and creativity, which enabled them "to settle into the interstices of a complex urban society".[18] These characteristics were certainly very marked in the Italians who came to Wales from the Ceno Valley. They brought to Wales very little that was based on their old rural way of life in Italy. They did not prepare Italian food in their cafés or restaurants, except for their own consumption at the back. Instead they gave the customers what they wanted and what could most easily be supplied. Oxo cubes, pork pies, beans on toast must have been as rare in Bardi as snow in August; and even the techniques for making ice-cream were picked up in Paris or London rather than in the hills around Bardi. They did not even look like people from a peasant background. Giovanni Conti, on his way from Cefn Fforest to search out premises in Newport in the 1930s, looked every bit a Milan banker, with his Anthony Eden hat and sober suit. Angelo Fecci in his dapper bow-tie would have looked equally at home in a New York bar as in his shop in Llanbraddach.[19]

It was what the Italians created, rather than what they brought from Bardi, that made most impact on the Welsh. The Temperance Bars, in particular, offered something new. They were warm and bright and cheerful. The owners were friendly and obliging. They provided an alternative to the public houses and, unlike the public houses in the 1920s and 1930s, they were open almost around the clock. They gave, particularly to the young, single, working man a service which the Welsh themselves, by their temperament, would never have provided. The Italians brought a certain élan; even the sweets they sold were, as Gwyn Thomas says, "very classy" things for the valleys. They were without a doubt a cut above the more prosaic Welsh corner shops.

The Wider Scene

It is not surprising, therefore, that the Italian community which began to be established in Wales at the end of the nineteenth century should, from the start, have been popular with the native population. To see whether this is unique to the *Bardigiani* in Wales, we need to look briefly at the experiences of other Italian immigrant groups. There were in fact two other groups in Wales which through geography or timing fall outside the main stream of this study: the Italian miners who were temporary residents in Cardiganshire around the year 1900, and the immigrants who came from all parts of Italy to work in the mines and tinplate works after the Second World War.

In 1898, a lead and zinc mine at Frongoch in Cardiganshire, which had been struggling to achieve profitability for at least twenty years, was taken over by a Belgian firm which imported Italian labour into the mine. The arrival of the Italians was followed by strikes and other disturbances. In November 1900, according to the *Mining Journal*, disputes between the two hundred and fifty Welshmen and two hundred Italians in the workforce were "of a serious nature, necessitating the presence of county police day and night, the tact of Chief-constable Evans alone keeping the Welsh miners in check". When several Italians became unwell it was assumed, without any evidence, that they had unwittingly introduced miner's anaemia into the mine. However, when samples were submitted by the government inspector, the fears proved to be unfounded. Even when the Welsh and the Italians were not in dispute, problems of language and communications added to the technical difficulties being encountered in the mine. The mine closed in December 1902, although the Italian labour seems to have been withdrawn, or at least considerably reduced in size, some time earlier. The 1901 census does not show any Italian presence in rural Wales on this scale, and other sources indicate that the workforce at Frongoch fell markedly between 1900 and 1901.[20]

After the Second World War, the tinplate industry in South Wales experienced a severe shortage of labour, particularly in the mill departments. After a failure to attract back those who had left the industry, and unsuccessful experiments in the employment of Poles and Irish, who tended not to stay, the industry turned in some desperation to Italy. Recruiting missions were sent to emigration centres in Naples, Milan and Genoa in the 1950s and some two thousand two hundred and fifty Italians were brought into the industry, of whom some one thousand and fifty remained in 1956 by which time the demand for labour had slackened. Some of the older works were closed down and the Italians found employment elsewhere. Some went back to Italy; others turned to the service sector and joined the café trade.

When they first arrived, these Italians were not well received in the tinplate industry. They were housed in an industrial hostel with other workers and the racial differences soon gave rise to problems, as did misunderstandings at work caused by language difficulties. A number returned quickly to Italy, but some remarkably patient work by the management and unions helped others to settle in. The experiment was judged to have been successful, in marked contrast to a similar attempt to employ Italians in the coal mines in South Wales and Yorkshire. This was met with considerable hostility by the miners who refused to work with them. The Italians, who had been housed in National Coal Board hostels, were angered by this turn of events and even turned on representatives of the tinplate industry who attempted to recruit them.[21]

We can see even sharper contrasts with the *Bardigiani* experience if we look outside Wales. We have already mentioned the low standing of early Italian immigrants in America; a more extreme example is, perhaps, France.

As we saw in earlier chapters, emigration from Italy to France, has a long history. Throughout the nineteenth century Italians flocked across into France looking for employment; at first they followed itinerant trades — shoe blacks, organ grinders, poodle clippers — but as France became more and more industrialised, Italians worked in the factories, on the building sites, in the docks, and in the mines, usually in a labouring capacity. The greatest concentrations were in the South of France: by 1928, Marseille alone had an Italian population well in excess of one hundred thousand.

The Italians were not generally popular with the French. In the factories and mines they were disliked by the French workforce because they accepted lower wages and displaced French workers. Their image was also tarnished by the activities of political anarchists who had been expelled from Italy, and who lost no opportunity to stir up trouble. This underlying resentment of Italians — which, in Italian eyes, bordered on hatred — came to a head in the salt mines at Aigues Mortes in 1893, when serious fighting broke out at one works and quickly spread to others, with the villagers joining in on the side of the French workers. Men roamed the streets with pickaxes, firearms and coshes and a battle raged for two days until it was broken up by the army. At least fifty were killed and one hundred and fifty wounded. This incident, and the anti-Italian riots which followed the assassination of the French President one year later, occurred at a time when the Bracchis, Bernis and Rabaiottis were settling with greater ease in Wales.[22]

The experiences of these three groups of Italians show, quite clearly, that the Italian characteristics of adaptability and creativity by themselves could not ensure a smooth transition to a new way of life. In Cardiganshire, where the viability of the mine was always in doubt, the Italians would have been seen as a real threat to employment. In France, too, the effect of the Italians on employment and wages created a degree of resentment which swamped any appeal the Italians might have had in other respects. In the tinplate works and coal mines of South Wales, employment itself was not at risk, but the arrival of Italians in large numbers was obviously seen as a danger to the existing working culture. All this reinforces the view expressed earlier that the relatively small numbers of *Bardigiani* in South Wales, their dispersal throughout the population, and their engagement in small businesses, played a large part in their assimilation into the native community. To test this further we should look at the Italian community in Scotland, which had much in common with the community in Wales.

As in Wales, the main influx of Italians into Scotland began around the turn of the century; again, as in Wales, they went mainly into catering, although with perhaps an even greater emphasis on ice-cream manufacture and sale than their compatriots in Wales. The Italians found their way to most parts of Scotland, but in contrast to Wales, they tended to settle in the main towns, especially in Glasgow and Edinburgh. Between 1891 and 1933, one third of all Italians in Scotland lived in Glasgow, which had its own 'Bardi': the majority of Glasgow Italians came from Barga in Tuscany and most of the English-speaking people in Barga today speak with a Glaswegian accent.

However, even in Glasgow there was no Italian ghetto; no Italian church, no Italian hospital: the Italian population, living mainly in rooms above shops, was well dispersed throughout the city. The Italian community which, as in Wales, was loosely knit, is today well integrated into the Scottish way of life.[23]

The Scots however seem to have been more reserved in their attitude to the early Italians than the Welsh. In her semi-autobiographical novel *My Friends from Cairnton*, Jane Duncan gives a picture of an Italian family in a town near Glasgow in the early 1920s. The industries of 'Cairnton' — that is not its real name — are

119

coalmining and quarrying:

> Mr Antonio Cervi was of a type to be found in every small Scottish town and in numbers in Scottish cities these days, an Italian who had brought with him from Italy the ability to make icecream in summer and fried fish and chips in winter, a flair for business and a great capacity for sheer hard work...
>
> In my mind, in those early days, the Caff, as I called it like everybody else, was confused with Aladdin's cave, for never had I seen a place of such glitter and gilt and sparkle and splendour. All the walls were of looking-glass and on the shelves against this stood the glass bottles and jars and boxes of different-coloured sweets...Mr Cervi did not trade in penny slabs of candy or penny toffee-apples...No. Mr Cervi sold chocolates by the half-pound box to courting couples on their way to the pictures...

But for all this splendour, "Cairnton did not approve of the Cervi family any more than it approved of anyone else from outside and, indeed, approved of them even less for they were so much 'no' like ither Folk' as to be utterly damned in Cairnton eyes".[24]

The café, with its glitter and gilt, and mirrors around the wall, had much in common with Italian establishments in Wales although, with its interior divided into "a series of booths", its ambience would have been different from that of a Welsh temperance bar. Nevertheless the similarities are marked. It is the insular nature of the people of 'Cairntown' at that time and their disapproval of outsiders which perhaps marks the difference between Scotland and Wales. There would be good reasons for this: there was a much stronger protestant ethic in Scotland, and a relative lack of mobility of the native population. This would encourage insularity. In sharp contrast to, say, the county of Glamorgan, a very high proportion of the population in Scotland was native born. Outsiders, apart from Irish workers in the coal mines who were also disapproved of, were comparatively rare and would find difficulty in fitting in. This, again, reinforces the view that the assimilation of immigrants into a community is easier when the native population is already in a fluid state and is expanding rapidly, as it was in Wales.

However, the factors we have so far identified with the *Bardigiani* equally applied to Jews who settled in the South Wales valleys at the end of the nineteenth century seeking refuge from the wave of pogroms in eastern Europe. They, too, were hard working. Their numbers were relatively small, probably no more than twice the number of Italians, and they were equally well dispersed. Like the Italians, they were small business men finding their place in an expanding population; and yet, unlike the Italians they were the victims of planned racial attack. On the evening of 19 August 1911, about two hundred men took to the streets in Tredegar and attacked and looted Jewish shops. Two days later similar disturbances occurred at Ebbw Vale and Rhymney and quickly spread down the valleys as far as Bargoed in the Rhymney valley and Cwm in the Ebbw vale. After a week of destruction, the riots died away as quickly as they began.[25]

Unlike the riots at Tonypandy in the previous year, when shops owned by the native Welsh were the prime targets, and Italians suffered only from spontaneous side actions, the riots in the Tredegar area were aimed specifically at the Jews. Analyses of these events[26] have shown that whatever other influences may have been present — local economic difficulties, the effects of strikes, the general increase in violence in the mining valleys — anti-Jewish feeling was the dominating factor. This dislike, which was not spontaneous, seems to have arisen from the nature of the businesses carried out by the Jews, particularly the alleged practice of some Jews to acquire house properties and then force up the rent. In fact, few, if any, of those caught up in the riots followed this practice. It was the perception of the Jews by the Welsh, rather than the reality, which dictated events.

Whether the Welsh perception of the Jews was coloured by the long debates on the evil of immigration which preceded the introduction of the Aliens Act only six years earlier, and the jingoistic books and pamphlets that were prevalent at the turn of the century, it is difficult to say. The Jews had been seen then by many politicians as a great threat to the British way of life; the Italians on the other hand emerged from these debates unscathed.

In the case of the Italian café keepers in South Wales, the way they were perceived by the native population, and the reality, seemed to coincide, and this, perhaps, owes much to the café way of life. Customers stayed in the cafés for hours on end and got to know the proprietors well. The Italians were seen as honest and friendly; they posed no threat; their services were enjoyed. By contrast, visits to, say, a Jewish pawnbroker's shop must have been furtive and unwelcome happenings, not calculated to endear the shopkeeper to his client, however much the service was needed. Similarly, the payment, or non-payment, of rent was more likely to be a source of friction rather than of joy.

From all these comparisons we can conclude that the assimilation of the *Bardigiani* in South Wales was, if not unique, at least unusual in its success. This was dependent on many factors, all of them important: the determination, drive and adaptability of the Italians; their inventiveness and flair for business; their choice of a trade which posed no threat to the employment of others, and which brought the Italians into close contact with the Welsh; their dispersal throughout the native population in relatively small numbers; the booming economy in South Wales when the Italians first arrived; and a fluid, rapidly expanding, cosmopolitan population. In this environment, the *Bardigiani* found their niche in the café trade. They seized their opportunities and made an impact on South Wales out of all proportion to their numbers.

Notes

Chapter 1

1. Ino Conti, Treharris, letter to the author, with notes, January 1987. His account draws on recollections of a long visit to the Ceno valley in 1933, when this form of agriculture was still practised. In 1986, Mr Conti took me to his ancestral home at Porelli, and to the nearby hamlet of Ronchi, now derelict (see plate 3), where evidence of this way of life can still be seen.
2. Martin Clark, *Modern Italy 1871-1982*, 1984, p.12. The summary of the Italian economy which follows is also based on this source (pp.12-36), with additional material from Christopher Seton-Watson, *Italy from Liberalism to Fascism*, 1967, D Mack Smith, *Italy*, 1959, and Lucio Sponza, *Italian Immigrants in Nineteenth-Century Britain: Realities and Images*, 1988.
3. Seton-Watson, *op. cit.*, p.80.
4. The description of the *Mezzadria* system is taken from Mack Smith, *op. cit.*, p.43.
5. Seton-Watson, *op. cit.*, p.83.
6. Ino Conti, Treharris.
7. Clark, *op. cit.*, p.36. The figures are taken from Italian census reports.
8. Clark, *op. cit.*, p.32.
9. *Encyclopaedia Britannica*, 15th edition, 1985: entry for 'ice cream'.
10. Clark, *op. cit.*, p.32.
11. J. D. Whelplay, *The Problem of Immigrants*, 1905, p.41.
12. Margaret Carlyle, *Modern Italy*, 1957, p.27.
13. Mack Smith, *op. cit.*, p.242.
14. Carlyle, *op. cit.*, p.28; Mack Smith, *op. cit.*, p.242.
15. Mack Smith, *op. cit.*, p.242.
16. Whelplay, *op. cit.*, p.239.
17. R. King, 'Italian Migration to Great Britain', *Geography*, Vol 62, 1977, p.177.
18. *Census of England and Wales*, HMSO, 1881 to 1931 inclusive.
19. *Parliamentary Papers, Report of the Royal Commission on Alien Immigration*, Cd 1741, 1903.
20. King, *op. cit.*, p.177.
21. J. Ronald Williams, 'The influence of foreign nationalities on the life of the people of Merthyr Tydfil', *The Sociological Review*, Vol 18, 1926, pp.148-152.
22. By inspection from *Guida Generale degli Italiani in Gran Bretagna*, London, 1939. Referred to hereafter as *Guida Generale*.
23. Sponza, *op. cit.*, p.11.
24. K. O. Morgan, *Rebirth of a Nation, 1981*, p.59.
25. T. Boyns, D. Thomas, C. Baber, 'The Iron, Steel and Tinplate Industries 1750-1914', *Glamorgan County History*, 1980, pp.97-129.
26. *Ibid.*, p.128.

27. G. M. Holmes, 'The South Wales Coal Industry 1850-1914', *Trans. Hon. Soc. Cymmrodorion*, 1976, p.183; J. Williams, 'The Coal Industry 1750-1914', *Glamorgan County History*, 1980, pp.181-187.
28. G.E. Jones, *Modern Wales*, 1984, p.175; Morgan, *op. cit.*, pp.66-67.
29. *Census of England and Wales*, 1871 to 1921 inclusive.
30. Dai Smith, *Wales! Wales?*, 1984, p.21; Jones, *op. cit.*, p.165.
31. *Census of England and Wales*, 1901.
32. Thomas Jones, *Rhymney Memories*, 1970, p.5.
33. *Ibid.*, p.56.
34. E. D. Lewis, *The Rhondda Valleys*, 1959, p.203.
35. Thomas Jones, *op. cit.*, p.62.
36. Bert Coombes, *These Poor Hands*, 1939, pp.27-28.
37. 'Ciao Charlie Rossi', BBC 2 television documentary, 25 August 1986. Produced by Paul Pierrot.
38. *Ibid*.
39. Millo Caffagnini, interviewed in Bardi, 1986
40. Sponza, *op. cit.*, pp.31-36.
41. *Ibid.*, p.40.
42. *Ibid.*, p.73-74.
43. RG 11. Census Returns (Holborn District, London) 1881.
44. Sponza, *op. cit.*, p17.
45. 'Ciao Charlie Rossi'; M Caffagnini, *Bardi: un paese per cento citta*, Bardi 1978, p.65, and several Welsh Italian correspondents.
46. 'The Bracchis of Bardi', BBC Radio 4 documentary, 25 January 1980. Produced by Herbert Williams.
47. Luigi ('Gino') Rabaiotti, interviewed in Swansea, May 1988, supplied the photograph and identified those in it, including his father, Luigi.
48. *Western Mail*, 8 January 1940. Peter Bracchi, a descendent of Giacomo Bracchi, also said in an interview in the 'Bracchis of Bardi' that Giacomo had lived in London before moving to Wales.
49. Home Office paper HO1, 'Certificates of Naturalisation, Index to Names', lists Giacomo Bracchi (Aberdare 1908) and Giovanni Berni (Neath 1910) amongst the very small number of Italians in the whole of England and Wales issued with naturalisation certificates before 1914.
50. *Guida Generale*, p.338.
51. Mario Opel, Neath, interviewed in Bardi 1986, told me that his father, Joseph, left Bardi in 1908 to work for Sidoli in Kenfig Hill. The dates of arrival of the Sidoli brothers were provided by Joe Carpanini of Glyn-corrwg in 1988.
52. Gino Assirati, Bargoed: letter to the author dated 16 January 1986.
53. The late Giovanni Conti, interviewed in 'The Bracchis of Bardi'. The date of his arrival was given to me by his wife, Maria, interviewed in Bassaleg in February 1986.
54. John Parker, *The Alien Land*, 1961, p.17. The introduction to the novel says that although the characters are "wholly fictitious", the events described "have a place in history".

55. *Ibid.*, pp.17-18. Descriptions given to me by other people (for example Mrs Maria Conti) confirm that this is an accurate picture of an early Italian café.

Chapter 2

1. Peter Bracchi in 'The Bracchis of Bardi'.
2. Paul Sidoli, Ebbw Vale. Telephone conversation, January 1986.
3. Sponza, *op. cit.*, pp. 71 and 99.
4. Luigi ('Gino') Rabaiotti, interviewed in Swansea, May 1988.
5. Marco Fulgoni, son of Giovanni, interviewed in Pontypridd, November 1986.
6. 'The Bracchis of Bardi'.
7. *Ibid.*
8. Mrs E. Spinetti, Abergavenny. Telephone conversation, October 1986.
9. *Parliamentary Debates,* 4th Series, Vol 133, 1904 and Vol 150, 1905. The brief description of previous Parliamentary interest in curbing the flow of aliens is taken from Lord Balfour's opening speech in the House of Lords debate on the second reading of the Aliens Bill, 28 July 1905 (Columns 749-755).
10. *Parliamentary Debates,* Vol 151 (Column 21).
11. *Parliamentary Debates,* Vol 133 (Column 1152).
12. Lucio Sponza - private communication based on Dr Sponza's examination of the Archivo del Comune di Borgotaro (Box for 1828, File 'Police', Comune di Bardi)'
13. Sponza, as cited above but from Archivo di Stato, Parma: Sottoprefettura di Borgotaro (Box 84, Folder 'Passports').
14. W. H. Wilkins, 'The Italian Aspect' in *The Destitute Alien in Great Britain,* [Ed] Arnold White, 1892, pp.146-151.
15. Ino Conti, Treharris, letter, January 1987.
16. Mario Opel, Neath, interviewed in Bardi 1986.
17. Gino Assirati, Bargoed, letters to the author, 16 and 28 January 1986.
18. John Conti, interviewed in Bassaleg, February 1986, described Newport as the graveyard of the Italians. Nevertheless, Giovanni Conti - John's father - and his family left Cefn Fforest in the 1930s and, against the trend, established the highly successful Empire Restaurant in Newport. See also the preface to this study and note 20 below.
19. Les Servini, interviewed in 'Another Valley', BBC 1 (Wales) 7 December 1986 (produced by Patrick Hannan).
20. Maria Conti, interviewed in Bassaleg, February 1986, with supplementary information from 'The Bracchis of Bardi'. This is the 'Mrs Conti' described in the preface as "hovering behind the counter" in her husband's shop in Cefn Fforest in the mid-1930s. It was a great pleasure for me to meet her again after an interval of more than fifty years.
21. Mrs Pierina Cordani, interviewed in Hengoed, April 1986.

22. Walter Haydn Davies, *Ups and Downs*, Christopher Davies, Swansea, 1975, pp.152-153.
23. J. W. Hopkins, *The Rise and Progress of the Temperance Movement* Templar Printing Works, Birmingham, 1905, pp.14-32.
24. W. R. Lambert, *Drink and Sobriety in Victorian Wales 1820-1895*, University of Wales Press, Cardiff, 1983, pp.214-223.
25. Parliamentary Papers, Session: 11 February-18 August 1890, Vol XL: 'Report of the Royal Commission appointed to inquire into the Operation of the Sunday Closing (Wales) Act, 1881', Cd 5994, *passim*. The evidence given by the Vicar of St John's Cardiff is recorded on p.72.
26. *Ibid*, p.xxix.
27. *Parliamentary Papers*, Session: 13 February-21 December 1906, Vol XIII: 'Minutes of Evidence taken before the Joint Select Committee on Sunday Trading', pp.114-116.
28. *Ibid*. pp.112-114.
29. Cd 5994 (see note 25), p.197, para 5988.
30. *Ibid*. 'List of Witnesses'.
31. Museum of London: caption to exhibits on temperance. The 'temperance public-houses' were overtaken in the late 1890s by the popular tea rooms of J. Lyons, and the Aerated Bread Company (ABC).
32. *The Rhondda Leader*, 5 February 1910. Reinecke's temperance bar boasted "the finest hot-water installation" and "absolutely perfect" sanitary and ventilation arrangements.
33. 'The Bracchis of Bardi'.
34. Marco Fulgoni, interviewed in Pontypridd, November 1986.

Chapter 3

1. John B. Hilling, *Cardiff and the Valleys*, London 1973, p.102.
2. *Western Mail*, 28 November 1904.
3. John Charles, *Pontypridd Historical Handbook*, Pontypridd 1920. The Rhondda was the source of much of the market trade in Pontypridd.
4. *The Times*, 26 June 1894. This issue also updates the position at the Albion colliery: "Before evening, nearly 230 bodies had been brought to bank, and of these all, with the exception of about 30, have been identified".
5. G. Carocci, *Storia d'Italia. Dall'unita ad Oggi*, Vol 4, Section II, 'L'Emigrazione', pp.535-541, 1975; also *The Times*, 22-30 August 1893, which the Italian historian uses as a major source.
6. *The Times*, 27 and 30 June 1894.
7. Marco Fulgoni and Ida Pini, interviewed in Pontypridd, 23 November 1986; *The Observer/Leader*, 12 December 1985 ('Express runs out of steam').
8. By inspection from *Guida Generale*.
9. Mrs Emilio Picarro (nee Pinchiaroli) interviewed in Mountain Ash, 30 May 1987. Mrs Picarro's father came from Bogotaro before the first world

war and had cafés in Caerphilly, Ynyshir and then Pontypridd.

10. See note 7.

11. E. D. Lewis, *The Rhondda Valleys*, Cardiff 1959, *passim*.

12. *Rhondda Leader*, 19 July 1919.

13. Lewis, *op. cit.*, pp.228-238.

14. *Census of England and Wales*, 1881, 1901 and 1911.

15. As quoted in a letter to the Secretary of State for Wales, from K.S. Hopkins (ed), *Rhondda: Past and Future*, Ferndale 1975, p.268.

16. Mrs Tina Cordani (see note 27).

17. T. S. Jenkins of Llwynypia: letters to the author, 10 August and 2 September 1986.

18. Lewis, *op. cit.*, pp.82-83 and 90. In 1916, the coal output of the 'Glamorgan' collieries was 905,000 tons compared to 595,000 tons from the Naval collieries.

19. Arnold Harrison: telephone conversation, September 1986. Mr Harrison, a former Town Clerk in the Rhondda, has a long association with a number of Italian families.

20. Lewis, *op.cit.*, pp.200-201.

21. G. M. Holmes, 'The South Wales Coal Industry 1880-1914', *Trans. Hon. Soc. Cymmrodorion* 1976, p.200; Lewis, *op. cit.*, p.201; Kenneth O. Morgan, *Wales 1880-1980*, London 1981, pp.146-147: Dai Smith, *Wales! Wales?*, London 1984, pp.66-75.

22. *The Rhondda Leader*, 12 November 1910.

23. *Ibid.*

24. See, for example, Deian Hopkin, 'The Llanelli Riots 1911', *The Welsh History Review*, Vol 11, No 4, 1983, esp. pp.489-90.

25. For a full account of the Tonypandy riots, and an analysis of the likely causes, see David Smith, 'Tonypandy 1910: Definition of Community', *Past and Present*, No 87, May 1980, pp.158-184.

26. See note 17 and the text to which it refers.

27. Mrs Tina Cordani (nee Melardi), interviewed in Aberaman, 1 December 1987. The information on the Bracchis and the detailed history of the Melardi family which follows is based on this interview.

28. Lewis, *op. cit.*, pp.83-84 and 104; Elizabeth Phillips, *History of the Pioneers of the Welsh Coalfield*, Cardiff 1925, pp.162-3; Holmes, *op. cit.*, p.202 (for the reference to the authority exercised by W.T. Lewis in his heyday).

29. This account of the history of T and E is taken from Owen Vernon Jones, *William Evans 1864-1934*, Porth (undated), *passim*, except for the specific reference to the reluctance of Italian cafés to retail the mineral waters, which was given to me orally by Aldo Bacchetta of Porth.

30. Aldo Bacchetta, letter dated 13 June 1986.

31. Maria Carpanini, Ino Conti, John Conti, Vic Restighini, Lily Spinetti, in interviews, 1986/7.

Chapter 4

1. Gwyn Thomas, 'The Dark Philosophers', collected with other stories in *The Sky of our Lives,* London 1972, pp.104-131.
2. *Ibid,* pp.106-108.
3. Elizabeth Wiskman, *Fascism in Italy: its Development and Influence,* London 1969, pp.8-9.
4. The *Guida Generale* shows that an Italian Fascist secretary - Dr Zanasi - worked in Cardiff and lived in Tredegar in 1939.
5. The following account of Benito Mussolini's early life and rise to power is taken, unless otherwise indicated, from Denis Mack Smith's biography, *Mussolini*, London 1969. For a very readable description of the main political parties of the time see Martin Clark, *Modern Italy 1871-1982,* pp.136-153. Although the socialist party was the largest single party after the 1919 and 1921 elections, a coalition of other parties formed the government on each occasion.
6. Clark, *op. cit.,* pp.245 and 271.
7. Peter M. Brown, 'A note on Fascism' included in the London edition of T. Carlo Levi's *Cristo si e fermato a Eboli* (Christ stopped at Eboli), London 1965, p.33.
8. FO 371 25210 (Foreign Office documents: Political, Western, Coordination): Memorandum prepared by Professor Bruno Foa, former legal adviser to the Consulate General and secretary to the British Chamber of Commerce in Naples.
9. Clark, *op. cit.,* p.273; Margaret Carlyle, *Modern Italy,* London 1957, p.28.
10. Mack Smith, *Italy,* Michigan 1959, p.242.
11. C. Cavalli, *Ricordi di un Emigrato,* Italy 1973, p.66.
12. Plate 15, taken against the background of a colliery, shows the pupils of an Italian school in the Rhondda proudly displaying the Italian flag.
13. Cavalli, *op. cit.,* p.67.
14. Mack Smith, *Mussolini*, p.53; *Guida Generale*, p.9-11.
15. The *Guida Generale,* from which we have quoted freely in this study, seems to have been compiled from the records of one or more of these organisations. Published in 1939 (year 'XVII' of the Fascist calender), its cover bears the fascist symbol, and the lists of names inside are prefaced by descriptions of the fascist organisation in London and its activities. It would be quite wrong, however, to assume that the Italians listed in the guide had any connection with, or even sympathy for, the fascist movement. Some did, but most are there because they happened to be engaged in these particular trades.
16. Mack Smith, *Mussolini*, pp.228-229; Clark, *op. cit.,* pp.281-282.
17. *Christ stopped at Eboli,* Italy/France 1979, based on Carlo Levi's book. One of the great classics of modern Italian cinema, directed by Francesco Rosi.
18. Mack Smith, *Mussolini*, p.229; Clark, *op. cit.,* p.282.

19. *The Times*, 3 October 1935.
20. *Western Mail*, Friday 4 October 1935.
21. *Western Mail*, Saturday 5 October 1935.
22. Cavalli, *op. cit.*, p.68; *Guida Generale*, p.328.
23. Joseph Opel, for example, was advised by a friendly police sergeant to become naturalised "because of the way things were going". He took the advice. (Mario Opel, interviewed in Bardi 1986.)
24. Clark, *op. cit.*, pp.282-285.
25. There are two excellent sources of information on the internment of 'enemy aliens' in wartime Britain: Francois Lafitte's *The Internment of Aliens*, London 1940, which was written as the events were unfolding, and Peter and Leni Gillman's *'Collar the Lot!'*, London 1980, which is based on considerable study of government papers and on interviews with internees. I have drawn freely on these books, checking where appropriate with the primary sources in the Public Records Office from which I also quote.
26. Gillman, *op. cit.*, pp.42-43.
27. FO 371 25210. This assessment of MI5's position is taken from the Snell Report on the inquiry into the sinking of the 'Arandora Star'.
28. *The Times*, for example, in its issue of 20 June 1940.
29. Gillman, *op. cit.*, p153.
30. FO 371 25210 (Snell Report).
31. 'Ciao Charlie Rossi', BBC 2, 25 August 1986.
32. 'Another Valley', BBC 1 (Wales), 7 December 1986.
33. *South Wales Evening Post*, 12 June 1940.
34. *Daily Mirror*, 27 April 1940, as quoted by Gillman, *op. cit.*, p150.
35. *South Wales Evening Post*, 11 June 1940.
36. *Western Mail*, 12 June 1940.
37. *Free Press and Rhondda Leader*, 8 June 1940 - a report of a court case. The two parties afterwards shook hands.
38. *Ibid*. 15 June 1940.
39. *South Wales Evening Post*, 11 June 1940.
40. Gillman, *op. cit.*, pp.97 and 156.
41. *Ibid*. p.225.
42. *Ibid*. pp.163-164 and 170.
43. Bert Rabaiotti, interviewed in 'Another Valley'; Angelo Moruzzi, interviewed in 'Ciao Charlie Rossi'.
44. FO 371 25210, 'Confidential Report of U. Limentari about his internment and the sinking of the SS Arandora Star.' (Written in early August 1940 and forwarded to the Foreign Office via the Labour Party.)
45. Gillman, *op. cit.*, p.156.
46. 'Another Valley.'
47. FO 371 25192, letter dated 19 June 1940 from the Home Secretary, Sir John Anderson, to the Foreign Secretary, Lord Halifax.
48. FO 916 2580 File KW5/5. Minutes of 'Conference on move of Prisoners of War and Internees to Canada, held at the War Office, Room 08 at 5pm on Monday June 17 1940'.

49. FO 371 25192, letter from Halifax to Anderson, 15 July 1940.
50. FO 371 25210, the Snell Report.
51. Gillman, *op. cit.*, pp.185-189, using information from the Blue Star Line and from a canteen manager who sailed on the 'Arandora Star.'
52. Ivor Duxbury, interviewed on 'Ciao Charlie Rossi'.
53. FO 371 25210. Limentani's written report on the sinking of the 'Arandora Star' has the advantage of having being compiled immediately after the event. I have therefore used it in preference to later oral accounts by other survivors (for example, those recorded in Gillman, *op. cit.*, and the two Welsh television programmes).
54. FO 371 25210. 'Embarkation List, Arandora Star', drawn up by the War Office. Foreign Office calculations, written in manuscript in the margins, revealed that out of a total of 712 Italians on board, 486 were lost and 226 saved. The figures for Germans lost were 175 out of a total of 478. The Italian losses were therefore proportionally much higher than the German. Having made their calculations, the Foreign Office entered a note of caution about their accuracy. The list shows, for example, that Limentani was lost whereas it was clear to the Foreign Office that he was very much alive.
55. FO 371 25192. Halifax to Anderson 15 July 1940: Anderson to Halifax, 19 July 1940.
56. Edda Conti, daughter of Ernesto Cordani, supplied the photograph. Ino Conti and Luigi Rabaiotti between them identified all in the picture as Welsh Italians (by letter and by interview).
57. Luigi ('Gino') Rabaiotti, interviewed in Swansea, May 1988.
58. FO 371 25210. War Cabinet Conclusion 284(40).
59. *Ibid*. The Snell Report.
60. *Ibid*. Letter from Harold Farquhar, Foreign Office.
61. *Ibid.*, Loraine to Sargent 25 November 1940.
62. Mack Smith, *Mussolini,* p.344.
63. *Ibid.* p.372.

Chapter 5

1. G.E. Jones, *Modern Wales,* 1984, pp.188-189; K.O. Morgan, *Rebirth of a Nation,* 1981, pp.308-318.
2. Morgan, *op. cit.*, p.347.
3. Tony Viazzani in 'Another Valley', 1986.
4. Millo Caffagnini, letter dated 23 June 1986. The figure of around 7,000 is also quoted in his book *Bardi: un paese per cento citta,* Bardi 1978.
5. Iolanda Rossi, interviewed in 'Ciao Charlie Rossi', 1986.
6. 'Today' programme, Radio 4, 16 May 1988.
7. 'The Bracchis of Bardi', Radio 4, 1980.
8. Ino Conti, 'Home Thoughts from Abroad', *Associazione Amici Val Ceno Gazetta,* October 1987.

9. Ino Conti, letter and notes, 9 January 1987.
10. 'The Bracchis of Bardi', 1980.
11. *Inciclopedia Italiana*, Milano 1930, entry for 'Bardi'.
12. Humbert S. Nelli, *From Immigrants to Ethnics: The Italian Americans*, Oxford 1983, p.vii.
13. *Census of England and Wales*, 1911.
14. Mrs Lily Spinetti (née Jones), wife of the late Giuseppe Spinetti, interviewed by telephone, 1986.
15. In 1907, Mr Walter Gardiner of Mountain Ash was one such helper, as he told Bernard Baldwin 80 years later (letter from Bernard Baldwin dated 5 March 1987).
16. Letter from Ethelyn Prankerd (née Reed) dated 27 January 1986.
17. Maria Conti, Tina Cordani and Ino Conti respectively provided these examples.
18. Lucio Sponza, *Italian Immigrants in Nineteenth Century Britain*, Leicester 1988, p.267.
19. Angelo Fecci's café was featured in 'Another Valley', showing him in bow tie.
20. David Bick, 'Frongoch Lead and Zinc Mine', *British Mining*, No 30 (The Northern Mine Research Society Sheffield), 1986, pp.19-21. The article quotes from contemporary sources including *Mining Journal* for 24 November 1900. There are conflicting figures for the size of the Italian workforce, which may well have been somewhat lower than that given in *Mining Journal*.
21. Leonard D. Matthews, 'Note on the Employment of Italians in the Tinplate Trade', unpublished article, Swansea 1960; also Gilbert and Tatler, *Immigrants, Minorities and Race Relations*, London 1984, which mentions in its introduction a drift away from the steel industry to catering.
22. See note 5 to Chapter 3.
23. Terri Colpi, 'The Italian Community in Glasgow, with special reference to Spacial Development', *Association of Teachers of Italian Journal*, No 29, 1979, pp.61-62; and Andrew Wilkin, 'Origins and Destinations of the Early Italo-Scots', pp.52-61 of the same issue of the journal: also *Censuses for Scotland*, 1901-1931.
24. Jane Duncan (Elizabeth Jane Cameron), *My Friends from Cairnton*, London 1966, pp.75-78.
25. Geoffrey Alderman, 'The anti-Jewish Riots of August 1911 in South Wales', *The Welsh History Review*, Cardiff, Vol 6 No 2, December 1972, pp.190-200.
26. Alderman, *op. cit.*; Colin Holmes, 'The Tredegar Riots of 1911: Anti-Jewish Disturbances in South Wales', *The Welsh History Review*, Cardiff, Vol 11 No 2, December 1982, pp.214-225.

Appendix 1

Number of Italian-born people in Wales and Monmouthshire. Figures in brackets show the number of naturalised British citizens. No county breakdown is available after the 1921 census.

Year	Place	Total	Male	Female
1871	Wales & Mon	243	220	23
	S. Wales	96	85	11
	N. Wales	36	32	4
	Monmouthshire	111	103	8
1881	Wales & Mon	580	543	37
	Glamorgan	455	429	26
	Monmouthshire	89	87	2
	Carmarthenshre	1	1	-
	Other W. Counties	35	26	9
1891	Wales & Mon.	567	510	57
	Glamorgan	511	461	50
	Monmouthshire	31	27	4
	Carmarthenshire	3	3	-
	Other W. Counties	22	19	3
1901	Wales & Mon.	927	811	115
	Glamorgan	684	602	82
	Monmouthshire	89	87	2
	Carmarthenshire	12	9	3
	Other W. Counties	141	122	19
1911	Wales & Mon.	1295	1055 (30)	240 (9)
	Glamorgan	833	675 (20)	158 (6)
	Monmouthshire	303	246 (4)	57 (3)
	Carmarthenshire	34	29	5
	Other W. Counties	125	105 (7)	20
1921	Wales & Mon.	1533	1105 (59)	428 (38)
	Glamorgan	995	703 (34)	294 (23)
	Monmouthshire	335	248 (18)	87 (9)
	Carmarthenshire	64	46	18 (2)
	Other W. Counties	137	108 (7)	29 (4)
1931	Wales	1394		

Appendix 2

Victims of the 'Arandora Star' from the Ceno Valley

Name	Place of Origin	Place of Arrest
Antoniazzi, Bartolomeo	Costageminiana	Gorseinon°
Basini, Bartolomeo	Pietrarada	Treherbert
Belli, Antonio	Bardi	Maesteg
Berni, Attilio	Bardi	Weston-s-Mare★
Carini, Francesco	Chiesabianca	Cilfynydd
Carini, Giuseppe	Chiesabianca	Ebbw Vale°
Carpanini, Giovanni	Vischeto	Blaenavon
Carpanini, Giuseppe	Carpana	Cwmcarn
Cavalli, Giovanni	Bardi	Neath
Chiappa, Emilio	Bardi	Bridgend
Conti, Giuseppe	Crederola	Treharris
Conti, Guido	Bardi	Newport
Franchi, Giacomo	Lezzara	New Tredegar
Fulgoni, Giacomo	Grezzo	Hirwaun
Fulgoni, Giovanni	Grezzo	Ferndale°
Gadeselli, Vincenzo	Costageminiana	London
Gazzi, Andrea	Grezzo	Gorseinon°
Gazzi, Francesco	Bardi	Pontnewydd
Gazzi, Lino	Grezzo	Ferndale
Gazzi, Francesco	Bardi	Not known
Gazzi, Vittorio	Grezzo	Aberbargoed
Giovanelli, Luigi	Casanova	Cardiff°
Marenghi, Giovanni	Casanova	Pontypridd
Marenghi, Luigi	Casanova	Not known
Mariani, Pietro	Grezzo	London
Menozzi, Gioacchino	Bardi	London
Minetti, Giacomo	Saliceto	Neath°
Moruzzi, Ernesto	Crederola	Neath
Moruzzi, Pierino	Gazzo	London
Moruzzi, Pietro	Crederola	Neath
Rabaiotti, Antonio	Grezzo	Newport
Rabaiotti, Bartolomeo	Crederola	Pontypridd
Rabaiotti, Domenico	Bardi	Ogmore Vale
Rabaiotti, Francesco	Bardi	Swansea
Rabaiotti, Luigi	Bardi	Swansea
Raggi, Luigi	Bardi	London
Ricci, Lazzaro	Gravago	Nelson
Rossi, Eugenio	Crederola	Mountain Ash
Rossi, Giovanni	Crederola	Hirwaun

Rossi, Luigi	Cacrovoli	Swansea
Sidoli, Giovanni	Grezzo	Cwmaman
Sidoli, Luigi	Grezzo	London
Solari, Luigi	Costalta	Neath
Spagna, Antonio	Gravago	Maesteg
Sterlini, Giuseppe	Lezzara	Wellington, Salop
Sterlini, Marco	Crederola	Tenby
Strinati, Giovanni	Costalta	Cwmaman
Tambini, Giovanni	Bardi	Newport
Zanelli, Ettore	Bardi	Tonypandy

* Lived in Wales before moving to Weston-super-Mare.
° Indicates some uncertainty about place of arrest.

Sources: Names and places of origin from the commemorative panels for the Arandora Star Memorial Chapel, Bardi; Place of arrest from private communication with Gino Rabaiotti. The chapel panels include the name of Bartolomeo Gazzi of Bardi and Ferndale, who died on the 'Ettrick' and not on the 'Arandora Star'.

Appendix 3

Italians in the Rhondda, c. 1938

Pontypridd
Antoniazzi, Ant., 27 Tram Road (but see Rabaiotti, Amedeo)
Antoniazzi, Pietro, Taff Street
Conti, L., Fish Restaurant, 25 Station Road
Cordani, Giov., Café, 9 High Street
Franchi, A., Café, 41 Taff Street
Fulgoni, G., Café, 68 Taff Street
Marenghi, G., Café, 33a Bridge Street
Marenghi, G., Café, 35 Mill Street
Orsi, Giov., Café Rest., 2 Station Road
Pinchiaroli, L., Café, 93 Taff Street
Rabaiotti, Amadeo, Café, 27 Tram Road
Rabaiotti, B., Café, 4 High Street
Rabaiotti, F., Café, 25 Station Road
Servini, Bart., Café, 29 Taff Street

Rhondda Fawr
Autenzio, F., 8 Club Row, Ystrad
Bacchetta, Serafino, Central Café, 3 Station Road, Porth
Balestrazzi, Dom. & Gius., Ice cream man. & tobacconist, 222 High Street, Treorchy
Basini, Ant., Fish Rest., 201 High Street, Treorchy
Basini Bros., Cafés, 103 Gwendoline Street, Treherbert (and branches)
Basini Bros., Café, 145 Bute Street, Treherbert
Bertorelli, Desiderio, Fish Rest., 42 Hannah Street, Porth
Bracchi, Francesco, Fish Bar, 190 Gelli Road, Pentre
Bracchi, Luigi, 35 Bedwlyn Road, Ystrad
Camisa, Gius., Ystrad Road, Pentre
Camisa, Vittorio, Café Confect., 39 Hannah Street, Porth
Carini, G., Café Confect., 13 Pandy Square, Tonypandy
Carpanini, Giov., Café, Pontypridd Road, Porth
Colombotti, E., Central Café, 111 Dunraven Street, Tonypandy
Coppolo, F., 65 Gelligeled Road, Ystrad
D'Esposito, S., 3 Cross Street, Penygraig
Emanuelli, G., 71 Tylacelyn Road, Penygraig
Figoni, Gius., Café Confect., 191 Gelli Road, Pentre
Fiorgione, Edoarde, Church Road, Ton Pentre
Gambarini, G. & Sons, Café Rest., Tynewydd Square, Porth
Gazzi, Daniele, 19 Llewellyn Street, Pentre
Ghisoni, A., Manufacturers Agent, 119 Trehafod Road, Trehafod
Giovannone, F., 46 Church Street, Pentre

Jafrate, Angelo, Café, The Square, Clydach
Malvisi, Jack, Turf Accountant, 123 Ynyshir Road, Ynyshir
Marchi, L., 81 Dumfries Street, Treorchy
Melardi, E., 5 De Winton Street, Tonypandy
Opel, Gius., 59 Llewellyn Street, Pentre
Rabaiotti, Ant., Café, 68 Tylacelyn Road, Penygraig
Rabaiotti Bros., Café Rest., 48 Ystrad Street, Pentre
Rea, Amedeo, 26 Eleanor Street, Tonypandy
Salvanelli, Seb., 59 Tylacelyn Road, Penygraig
Servini, G. & Sons, Café, Empire Buildings, Tonypandy
Sidoli, G., Café Confect., 212 High Street, Treorchy
Strinati, C., Café, 149 Bute Street, Treherbert
Tadecicco, G., Cafés, 135 & 147 Bute Street, Treorchy
Tanzi Bondini, O., 59 Llewellyn Street, Pentre (but see, Opel, Gius.)
Zanelli, E., Central rest., 109 Dunraven Street, Tonypandy

Rhondda Fach
Albertelli, Antonio, 24 Edward Street(?), Maerdy (but see Giudici)
Bacigalupo, Gius., Wholesale Confect. & Tobacconist, 61 High Street,
    Ferndale
Bertorelli, Giov., Fish Rest., 39 Duffryn Street, Ferndale
Caffarelli, Ant., 163 East Road, Tylorstown
Cavaciuti, Dom., 5 James Street, Maerdy
Fecchi, G., Express Café, 32 High Street, Ferndale
Gambarini, G., Fish Rest., 12 The Strand, Ferndale
Gambarini, Pietro, 7 Ceridwen Street, Maerdy
Gazzi, Lino, Café Confect., 34 High Street, Ferndale
Giudici, Ant., 24 Edward Road(?), Maerdy (but see Albertelli)
Maestri, Ant., Café Confect., 35 Ynyshir Road, Ynyshir
Pesci, Serafino, Fish Bar, 49 High Street, Ferndale

Source: the *Guida Generale*

Bibliography

Notes of Interviews

With first and second generation Italians in Wales: Aldo Bacchetta, Ron Bacchetta, Serafino Bacchetta, Giuseppe Carpanini, Maria Carpanini, Edda Conti, Ino Conti, John Conti, Maria Conti, Pierina Cordani, Tina Cordani, Alma Cushion, Marco Fulgoni, Mario Opel, Mrs Emilio Picarro, Ida Pini Luigi ('Gino') Rabaiotti, Vic Resteghini.
Others: Millo Caffagnini, Lily Spinetti (by telephone).

Letters to the Author

From: Gino Assirati, Aldo Bacchetta, Bernard Baldwin, Ino Conti, Alma Cushion, Arnold Harrison, T.S. Jenkins, Ethelyn Prankerd, Luigi ('Gino') Rabaiotti.

Official Reports

Censuses of England and Wales, 1871–1931
Censuses for Scotland, 1901-1931
Hansard, *Parliamentary Debates*, 4th Series, 1904 and 1905
'Minutes of Evidence taken before the Joint Select Committee on Sunday Trading': *Parliamentary Papers*, 1906, vol. XIII
'Report of the Royal Commission appointed to inquire into the Operation of the Sunday Closing (Wales) Act, 1817': *Parliamentary Papers*, 1890, vol. XL
'Report on the Royal Commission on Alien Immigration': Cmd 1741, *Parliamentary Papers*, H of C, 1903

Papers in the Public Records Office

RG 11: Enumerator's Census Returns, 1881
FO 371 25192, FO 371 25210: Foreign Office policy files 1939-45
FO 916 2580: Miscellaneous files on internment, 1940
HO 1: 'Certificates of Naturalisation: Index to Names'

Works of Reference

Enciclopedia Italiana, Milano 1930
Guida Generale degli Italiani in Gran Bretagna, London 1939
Encyclopaedia Britannica, 1985

Newspapers and Periodicals

Aberdare Leader
Daily Mirror
Free Press and Rhonnda Leader
Gazzetta (Associazione Amici Val Ceno)
Merthyr Express
Radio Times
Rhondda Leader
South Wales Echo
South Wales Evening Post
The Times
Western Mail

Unpublished Theses

Green, David R., 'The Stability of Immigrant Communities: Little Italy in Nineteenth Century London', Undergraduate Dissertation, Pembroke College Oxford, 1976

Sponza, Lucio, 'The Italian Poor in Nineteenth Century Britain', PhD, University of London, 1984

Contemporary Books and Pamphlets

Armfelt, E., 'Italy in London', in *Living London*, G.R. Sims (ed), 1902

Hopkins, J.W., *The Rise and Progress of the Temperance Movement*, Birmingham, 1905

Lafitte, F., *The Internment of Aliens*, Harmondsworth, 1940

Whelplay, J.D., *The Problem of Immigrants*, London 1905

White, Arnold (ed), 'The Influence of Foreign Nationalities on the Life of the People of Merthyr Tydfil', *The Sociological Review*, vol. 18, 1926

Biography and Memoirs

Cavalli, C, *Ricordi di un Emigrato*, Italy, 1973

Coombes, Bert L., *These Poor Hands*, London, 1939

Davies, Walter Haydn, *Ups and Downs*, Swansea, 1975

Jones, Owen Vernon, *Williams Evans 1864-1934*, Porth, no date

Jones, Thomas, *Rhymney Memories*, London, 1970

Mack Smith, Denis, *Mussolini*, London, 1969

Skidelsky, Robert, *Oswald Moseley*, London, 1975

Histories and Surveys

A. General

Carlyle, Margaret, *Modern Italy*, London, 1957
Carocci, G. (ed), *Storia d'Italia. Dall'Unità ad Oggi*, Turin, 1975
Clark, Martin, *Modern Italy 1871-1982*, London, 1984
Jones, G.E., *Modern Wales*, Cambridge, 1984
Mack Smith, Denis, *Italy*, London, 1959
Morgan, K.O., *Rebirth of a Nation, Wales 1880-1980*, Oxford, 1981
Seton-Watson, Christopher, *Italy from Liberalism to Fascism*, London, 1967
Smith, Dai, *Wales! Wales?*, London, 1984

B. Politics

Brown, Peter M., 'A Note on Fascism' in Carlo Levi's *Cristo si è fermato a Eboli*, London edition, 1965
Cassels, Alan, *Fascist Italy*, London, 1969
Cross, Colin, *The Fascists in Britain*, London, 1961
Hamilton, Alastair, *The Appeal of Fascism*, London 1975
Wiskmann, Elizabeth, *Fascism in Italy: its Development and Influence*, London, 1969

C. Industrial, Economic and Social

Aderman, Geoffrey, 'The Anti-Jewish Riots of August 1911 in South Wales', *The Welsh History Review*, Cardiff, vol.6 no.2 December 1972, pp. 190-200
Baldwin, Bernard, *Mountain Ash Remembered*, Cowbridge, 1984
Bick, David, 'Frongoch Lead and Zinc Mine', *British Mining*, no.30 (The Northern Mine Research Society, Sheffield), 1986.
Boyns, T., Thomas, D., Baber, C., 'The Iron, Steel and Tinplate Industries 1750-1914', *Glamorgan County History*, vol.V, Cardiff, 1980
Caffagnini, Millo, *Bardi: un paese per cento città*, Bardi, 1986
Charles, John, *Pontypridd Historical Handbook*, Pontypridd, 1920
Hall, Basil, 'The Welsh Revival of 1904-05: A Critique' in *Popular Belief and Practice*, Studies in Church History, vol.8, 1972
Hanson, J. Ivor, *Profile of a Welsh Town*, Swansea, 1968
Hilling, John B., *Cardiff and the Valleys*, London, 1973
Holmes, Colin 'The Tredegar Riots of 1911', *The Welsh History Review*, vol.11 no.4, 1983
Holmes, G.M., 'The South Wales Coal Industry 1880-1914', *Trans. Hon. Soc. Cymmrodorion*, London, 1986
Hopkin, Deian, 'The Llanelli Riots, 1911', *The Welsh History Review*, vol.11 no.4, 1983
Hopkins, K.S. (ed), *Rhondda: Past and Future*, Ferndale 1975

Lambert, W.R., *Drink and Sobriety in Victorian Wales 1820-1895*, Cardiff, 1983

Lewis, E.D., *The Rhondda Valleys*, Cardiff, 1959

Matthews, Leonard D., 'Note on Employment of Italians in the Tinplate Trade', Unpublished Article, Swansea, 1960 (kindly provided by Dafydd Llyr James of the Welsh Industrial and Maritime Museum)

Phillips, Elizabeth, *History of the Pioneers of the Welsh Coalfield*, Cardiff, 1925

Smith, David, 'Tonypandy 1910: Definition of Community', *Past and Present, no.87, May 1980*

Williams, C.R., 'The Welsh Religious Revival, 1904–05', *The British Journal of Sociology*, vol.III, 1952

Williams, J., 'The Coal Industry 1750-1914', *Glamorgan County History*, vol.V, Cardiff 1980

Migration and Internment
(see also Contemporary Books)

Bacchetta, Lawrence, 'Italian Immigration to South Wales', *Link*, Issue 45, Cardiff, 1985

Carrier, N.H. & Jeffrey, J.R., *External Migration: A Study of the Available Statistics*, London, 1953

Colpi, Terri, 'The Italian Community in Glasgow', *Association of Teachers of Italian Journal*, no.29, 1979

Colpi, Terri, *The Italian Factor*, Edinburgh, 1991

Colpi, Terri, *Italians Forward*, Edinburgh, 1991

Gillman, Peter & Leni, *Collar the Lot!*, London, 1980

King, R., 'Italian Migration to Great Britain', *Geography*, vol.62, 1977

Marin, Umberto, *Italiani in Gran Bretagna*, Rome, 1975

Nelli, Humbert S., *From Immigrants to Ethnics*, Oxford, 1983

Sponza, Lucio, *Italian Immigrants in Nineteenth Century Britain: Realities and Images*, Leicester 1988

Wilkin, Andrew, 'Origins and destinations of the Early Italo-Scots', *Association of Teachers of Italian Journal*, no.29, 1979

Novels

Duncan, Jane, *My Friends from Cairnton*, London, 1966

Parker, John, *The Alien Land*, Dublin, 1961

Thomas, Gwyn, *The Sky of Our Lives*, London, 1972

Radio and Television
(in chronological order)

'The Bracchis of Bardi', Radio 4, 25 January 1980 (compiled, presented and produced by Herbert Williams)
'Ciao Charlie Rossi', BBC 2, 25 August 1986 (produced by Paul Pierrot; narrated by Victor Spinetti)
'Another Valley', BBC 1 (Wales), 7 December 1986 (written, produced and presented by Patrick Hannan)
'Dangerous Characters', Channel 4, 26 & 29 July 1987 (Alfio Bernabei)

Film

'Christ stopped at Eboli', Italy/France, 1979 (directed by Francesco Rosi)

Acknowledgements

Illustrations

Thanks are due to: the Bacchetta family (17, 18); Bernard Baldwin (8); British Library (9); Edda Conti (23); Ino Conti (4, 5, 12); Marco Fulgoni (7, 13, 14, 15, 16); the Hulton Picture Library (20); Gino Rabaiotti (6); Vic Resteghini (19); the Ricci family (10, 11).

Extracts

The Estate of Walter Haydn Davies for the passages from *Ups and Downs* (Swansea, Christopher Davies Publishers, 1975); The Estate of Gwyn Thomas for the passages from 'The Dark Philosophers'; the Controller of Her Majesty's Stationary Office for extracts from papers in the custody of the Public Records Office.